SOLOMON

BIBLE STUDY GUIDE

From the Bible-teaching ministry of

Charles R. Swindoll

INSIGHT FOR LIVING

Charles R. Swindoll is a graduate of Dallas Theological Seminary and has served in pastorates for more than twenty-three years, including churches in Texas, New England, and California. Since 1971 he has served as senior pastor of the First Evangelical Free Church of Fullerton, California. Chuck's radio program, "Insight for Living," began in 1979. In addition to his church and radio ministries, Chuck has authored twenty-one books and numerous booklets on a variety of subjects.

Based on the outlines of Chuck's sermons, the study guide text is coauthored by Ken Gire, Jr., a graduate of Texas Christian University and Dallas Theological Seminary. The Living Insights are written by Bill Butterworth, a graduate of Florida Bible College, Dallas Theological Seminary, and Florida Atlantic University. Ken Gire, Jr., is presently the director of the educational products department at Insight for Living, and Bill Butterworth is currently the director of counseling ministries.

Editor in Chief:	Cynthia Swindoll
Coauthor of Text:	Ken Gire, Jr.
Author of Living Insights:	Bill Butterworth
Editorial Assistant:	Julie Martin
Copy Manager:	Jac La Tour
Senior Copy Assistant:	Jane Gillis
Copy Assistant:	Wendy Peterson
Director, Communications Division:	Carla Beck
Project Manager:	Nina Paris
Art Director:	Becky Englund
Production Artists:	Kathi Hilaski and Trisha Smith
Typographer:	Bob Haskins
Calligrapher:	David Acquistapace
Cover:	Painting by J. James Tissot, *Solomon Is Made King*
Print Production Manager:	Deedee Snyder
Printer:	Frye and Smith

ISBN 0-8499-8289-8

Ordering Information

An album that contains eight messages on four cassettes and corresponds to this study guide may be purchased through Insight for Living, Post Office Box 4444, Fullerton, California 92634. For ordering information and a current catalog, please write our office or call (714) 870-9161.

Canadian residents may obtain a catalog and ordering information through Insight for Living Ministries, Post Office Box 2510, Vancouver, British Columbia, Canada V6B 3W7, (604) 272-5811. Overseas residents should direct their correspondence to our Fullerton office.

If you wish to order by Visa or MasterCard, you are welcome to use our toll-free number, (800) 772-8888, Monday through Friday between the hours of 8:30 A.M. and 4:00 P.M., Pacific time. This number may be used anywhere in the continental United States excluding Alaska, California, and Hawaii. Orders from those areas can be made by calling our general office number, (714) 870-9161.

Table of Contents

Stepping into Big Sandals 1

Solomon in Living Color 7

Signs of Erosion 14

When the Heart Is Turned Away 22

How God Deals with Defiance 30

Sound Advice from an Old Rebel 37

A Plea for Godliness 43

Needed: A Godly Mind 49

Books for Probing Further 55

Acknowledgments 58

Ordering Information/Order Form 59

Solomon

Erosion is not limited to soil along the banks of a river. It can happen in life as well. Slow and silent like a stream, it sweeps away character a grain of sand at a time. From a distance, the landscape appears so tranquil and serene, but a closer look reveals the surging washout of integrity and morality.

So it was with Solomon. Born with all the benefits, blessed with a bright, creative mind and keen abilities, the man who became king also became a fool. Call it whatever you wish—sowing wild oats, mid-life crisis, spiritual defection, or just plain carnality—Solomon's passions broke their banks in a flood of immorality and idolatry. And for the rest of his life, he was busy mopping up the consequences.

From his gold crown to his clay feet, Solomon is thoroughly examined in the first six lessons. Not only do they depict his rich-and-famous lifestyle, but his subsequent moral bankruptcy as well. And lest we think we stand tall and upright by comparison, there are also two New Testament studies to keep us on our knees.

Chuck Swindoll

Putting Truth into Action

Knowledge apart from application falls short of God's desire for His children. Knowledge must result in change and growth. Consequently, we have constructed this Bible study guide with these purposes in mind: (1) to stimulate discovery, (2) to increase understanding, and (3) to encourage application.

At the end of each lesson is a section called **Living Insights.** *There you'll be given assistance in further Bible study, thoughtful interaction, and personal appropriation. This is the place where the lesson is fitted with shoe leather for your walk through the varied experiences of life.*

It's our hope that you'll discover numerous ways to use this tool. Some useful avenues we would suggest are personal meditation, joint discovery, and discussion with your spouse, family, work associates, friends, or neighbors. The study guide is also practical for church classes and, of course, as a study aid for the "Insight for Living" radio broadcast.

In order to derive the greatest benefit from this process, we suggest that you record your responses to the lessons in a notebook where writing space is plentiful. In view of the kinds of questions asked, your notebook may become a journal filled with your many discoveries and commitments. We anticipate that you will find yourself returning to it periodically for review and encouragement.

Ken Gire, Jr.
Coauthor of Text

Bill Butterworth
Author of Living Insights

SOLOMON

Stepping into Big Sandals

1 Kings 1, 2 Chronicles 1–9

Compared to Solomon, the "Lifestyles of the Rich and Famous" look like life on skid row. Their "champagne wishes" and "caviar dreams" stack up like city dump garbage next to the opulent display of his prosperity and power. Under Solomon, Jerusalem glistened like a brilliant gem in the golden setting between the liquid sapphire of the Mediterranean and the mineral-rich sparkle of the Dead Sea. This scintillating jewel was the central stone of the empire, where peace radiantly shined for forty years. Indeed, during his reign, Jerusalem was "a city set on a hill"—a light to the world. But Solomon's renown went beyond his wealth and extended to his wisdom as well. His fame spilled over the brimmed borders of Israel to inundate the entire Middle East. So incredible were the reports that the queen of Sheba herself journeyed from her kingdom in Africa to verify the source of this flood of rumors. Her breath was literally taken away when she saw Solomon's wisdom and glory.

> Then she said to the king, "It was a true report which I heard in my own land about your words and your wisdom. Nevertheless I did not believe their reports until I came and my eyes had seen it. And behold, the half of the greatness of your wisdom was not told me. You surpass the report that I heard." (2 Chron. 9:5–6)

News of Solomon's greatness still circulated in Israel during the time of Christ. In Matthew, Jesus speaks both of Solomon's glory (6:29) and of the greatness of his wisdom (12:42). Even today, Solomon's glory still gilds our perception. It is easy to envy the lifestyles of the rich and famous—especially Solomon's. There is much to eschew about his life—his eroding character, his errant ways. But there is also much to emulate.

I. Long Live the King (1 Kings 1:28–34)

In filling his father's royal shoes, Solomon was stepping into big sandals. But with David's deathbed blessing, Solomon's reign got off on the right foot. With the clarion call "Long live King Solomon!" a golden age of peace and prosperity stepped through the gates of Jerusalem. An age upon whose shoulders sat a young king who had been groomed for the throne since his boyhood.

1

A. His birth and name. After the storm of David's adultery with Bathsheba; in the wake of deception, murder, and cover-up (2 Sam. 11–12); and after a period of withering health and misery (Ps. 32), a calm came in the form of a son.

> Then David comforted his wife Bathsheba, and went in to her and lay with her; and she gave birth to a son, and he named him Solomon.[1] Now the Lord loved him and sent word through Nathan the prophet, and he named him Jedidiah[2] for the Lord's sake. (2 Sam. 12:24–25)

B. His childhood and training. Since God used Nathan to confer a special name upon Solomon, it is possible that the prophet was the young boy's tutor. Doubtless, however, Solomon's impressionable ears picked up other messages that loitered around his home—messages noting wickedness, tension, pride, and deception: Amnon's rape of his half-sister Tamar, Absalom's rebellion, David's sin of numbering the people, the political intrigue of Joab and Adonijah. And, as rumors die hard, hushed whispers of his father's checkered past probably still echoed through the marbled halls of the king's palace where Solomon grew up.

C. His inauguration and reign. Prosperity, loyalty, and majesty were the hallmarks of Solomon's reign.

> Then Solomon sat on the throne of the Lord as king instead of David his father; and he prospered, and all Israel obeyed him. And all the officials, the mighty men, and also all the sons of King David pledged allegiance to King Solomon. And the Lord highly exalted Solomon in the sight of all Israel, and bestowed on him royal majesty which had not been on any king before him in Israel. (1 Chron. 29:23–25)

For forty years, from about 970–930 B.C., Solomon sat on the throne of a united Israel, where all the people "lived in safety, every man under his vine and his fig tree, from Dan even to Beersheba, all the days of Solomon" (1 Kings 4:25).

II. "The Lord Was with Him" (2 Chronicles 1, 1 Kings 4)

During Solomon's reign God showered him with the blessings of wisdom, knowledge, discernment, strength, riches, fame, vision, and skill.

A. Giving him wisdom and knowledge (2 Chron. 1:7–12, 9:1–8, 22–23). At a time when Solomon's heart was tender toward God, a solitary pact between the two took place.

---

1. The Hebrew word for Solomon—*shelomoh*—comes from the root *shalom,* which means "peace."

2. The name Jedidiah means "loved by Jehovah."

In that night God appeared to Solomon and said to him, "Ask what I shall give you." And Solomon said to God, "Thou hast dealt with my father David with great lovingkindness, and hast made me king in his place. Now, O Lord God, Thy promise to my father David is fulfilled; for Thou hast made me king over a people as numerous as the dust of the earth. Give me now wisdom and knowledge, that I may go out and come in before this people; for who can rule this great people of Thine?" And God said to Solomon, "Because you had this in mind, and did not ask for riches, wealth, or honor, or the life of those who hate you, nor have you even asked for long life, but you have asked for yourself wisdom and knowledge, that you may rule My people, over whom I have made you king, wisdom and knowledge have been granted to you. And I will give you riches and wealth and honor, such as none of the kings who were before you has possessed, nor those who will come after you." (1:7–12)

Wisdom to Rule

Proverbs, written largely by Solomon, is a prism through which wisdom shines and refracts a rainbow of multi-hued meanings. One of these shadings is found in chapter 8, where wisdom is personified as a woman calling in the street. We are told that she "is better than jewels; / And all desirable things can not compare with her" (v. 11) . . . that prudence, knowledge, and discretion are her roommates (v. 12) . . . that by her "kings reign, / And rulers decree justice" (v. 15) . . . that "riches and honor" accompany her (v. 18) . . . and that he who finds her "obtains favor from the Lord" (v. 35). God may not have entrusted you with a great kingdom to rule as He did with Solomon, but He has entrusted *some* of His people to you—your family. Admittedly, it is a small kingdom. Then again, so was Bethlehem. Yet out of Bethlehem came the Savior of the world (Matt. 2:1–6)!

B. Giving him discernment and strength (1 Kings 4:29–34).
Besides having administrative gifts, Solomon was a poet, song-writer, and a lover of nature.

Now God gave Solomon wisdom and very great discernment and breadth of mind, like the sand that is on the seashore. And Solomon's wisdom surpassed the wisdom of all the sons of the east and all the wisdom of Egypt. For he was wiser than all men,... and his fame was known in all the surrounding nations. He also spoke 3,000 proverbs, and his songs were 1,005. And he spoke of trees, from the cedar that is in Lebanon even to the hyssop that grows on the wall; he spoke also of animals and birds and creeping things and fish. And men came from all peoples to hear the wisdom of Solomon, from all the kings of the earth who had heard of his wisdom.[3]

C. Giving him riches and fame (1 Kings 4:20–27, 10:14–22). Solomon's wealth was made up of a diversified portfolio of income, assets, and gifts.

Judah and Israel were as numerous as the sand that is on the seashore in abundance; they were eating and drinking and rejoicing. Now Solomon ruled over all the kingdoms from the River to the land of the Philistines and to the border of Egypt; they brought tribute and served Solomon all the days of his life. And Solomon's provision for one day was thirty kors[4] of fine flour and sixty kors of meal, ten fat oxen, twenty pasture-fed oxen, a hundred sheep besides deer, gazelles, roebucks, and fattened fowl. For he had dominion over everything west of the River, from Tiphsah even to Gaza, over all the kings west of the River; and he had peace on all sides around about him. So Judah and Israel lived in safety, every man under his vine and his fig tree, from Dan even to Beersheba, all the days of Solomon. And Solomon had 40,000 stalls of horses for his chariots, and 12,000 horsemen. And those deputies provided for King Solomon and all who came to King Solomon's table, each in his month; they left nothing lacking. (4:20–27)

"The king made silver as common as stones in Jerusalem" (10:27), but for his palace he used only the finest gold.

Now the weight of gold which came in to Solomon in one year was 666 talents[5] of gold, besides that from the traders and the wares of the merchants and

---

3. A classic example of his wisdom is found in the familiar passage of 1 Kings 3:16–28 where he settles a dispute between two women claiming to be the mother of the same child.

4. A kor was equivalent to ten bushels.

5. Six hundred sixty-six talents amounted to nearly 800,000 ounces.

4

all the kings of the Arabs and the governors of the country. And King Solomon made 200 large shields of beaten gold, using 600 shekels of gold on each large shield. And he made 300 shields of beaten gold, using three minas of gold on each shield, and the king put them in the house of the forest of Lebanon. Moreover, the king made a great throne of ivory and overlaid it with refined gold. There were six steps to the throne and a round top to the throne at its rear, and arms on each side of the seat, and two lions standing beside the arms. And twelve lions were standing there on the six steps on the one side and on the other; nothing like it was made for any other kingdom. And all King Solomon's drinking vessels were of gold, and all the vessels of the house of the forest of Lebanon were of pure gold. None was of silver; it was not considered valuable in the days of Solomon. For the king had at sea the ships of Tarshish with the ships of Hiram; once every three years the ships of Tarshish came bringing gold and silver, ivory and apes and peacocks. (10:14–22)

D. Giving him vision and skill (1 Kings 10:23–24). Solomon's reputation stretched across continents and brought back hungry audiences eager to catch the morsels of wisdom that fell from his lips.

So King Solomon became greater than all the kings of the earth in riches and in wisdom. And all the earth was seeking the presence of Solomon, to hear his wisdom which God had put in his heart.

III. "Forget None of His Benefits" (Psalm 103:1–2)

Obviously, Solomon was uniquely gifted. And it's human nature, when abundantly blessed, to forget the source of our benefits. An echo from Solomon's father, David, exhorts us in Psalm 103.

Bless the Lord, O my soul;
And all that is within me, bless His holy name.
Bless the Lord, O my soul,
And forget none of His benefits.

A Concluding Application

Israel did it...Solomon did it...we do it, daily: *forget*. When Israel entered the Promised Land, they *forgot* that it was God who had brought them there. God's warning to them, however, was clear:

5

> "But you shall remember the Lord your God, for it is He who is giving you power to make wealth." (Deut. 8:18a)
>
> Solomon restates this truth in Proverbs:
>
> It is the blessing of the Lord that makes rich. (10:22a)
>
> Sadly, Solomon failed to heed his own wisdom in his later reign. His abundance slowly inhibited his dependence on God. He became self-sufficient . . . his appetite, sated . . . and he soon forgot God. "Hunger is the best cook," or so the ancient Chinese proverb goes, because it is the hungry palate whose taste buds are sensitized to each subtle nuance of flavor, and is most aware of the hand that feeds it. It is the sated palate that is dull, pushes away the plate, and loses a taste for thankfulness. Carve out a slice of time to take a personal inventory. Count your blessings. Thank God for the peanut butter and crackers as well as for the steak in your life. "Forget none of His benefits"—because *forgetting* is the first step to *falling away.*

 Living Insights

Study One

Solomon's request for wisdom is recorded in 2 Chronicles 1:7–12. It can also be found in 1 Kings 3:5–14. Let's compare and contrast these two passages.

- Observe and list five similarities between the two passages (key facts, key words, order of events, and so forth).
- List three observations unique to 2 Chronicles 1:7–12.
- List three observations unique to 1 Kings 3:5–14.
- Let's personalize this. If God were to say to you, "Ask what you wish Me to give you," how would you respond? Don't be too quick to answer; think it through carefully.

 Living Insights

Study Two

Psalm 103 exhorts us to reflect on our benefits. Take some time to count your blessings, and remember to give thanks to God for them.

- List several ways you can further cultivate the blessing of a keen mind.
- How do you feel about the comforts with which God has blessed you? Undeserving? Humbled? Grateful? Guilty? Content? Dissatisfied? Apathetic? Joyful? Expand on your feelings.

Solomon in Living Color
Selected Scripture

Actors often get typecast into certain roles. Edward G. Robinson, for example, became typecast as a gangster. Similarly, Boris Karloff and Vincent Price were typecast for sinister parts in scary movies. And after *Dracula,* one wonders if Bela Lugosi was ever considered for the lead of a serious, romantic drama—he was forever typecast into vampirish roles. Sometimes we do that with people in real life. Thomas was a faithful disciple of Jesus for three long, hard years. Yet because of one moment of skepticism after the Resurrection, we have typecast him as Doubting Thomas. Solomon, too, has been unfairly dealt with by biblical historians. Most focus on his later, declining years, as if his entire life were one massive shipwreck. However, as we read the preface to his biography, we find the opposite—a young, eager king with a tender heart for the things of the Lord.

I. Solomon—Man of God
In the early stages of Solomon's reign, it was explicitly clear that God was with him.

> Now Solomon the son of David established himself securely over his kingdom, and the Lord his God was with him and exalted him greatly. (2 Chron. 1:1)

Solomon's *private* response to the Father was one of childlike dependence.

> "And now, O Lord my God, Thou hast made Thy servant king in place of my father David, yet I am but a little child; I do not know how to go out or come in. And Thy servant is in the midst of Thy people which Thou hast chosen, a great people who cannot be numbered or counted for multitude. So give Thy servant an understanding heart to judge Thy people to discern between good and evil. For who is able to judge this great people of Thine?" (1 Kings 3:7–9)

As a natural outgrowth of his private relationship with God, Solomon's *public* confession of faith was unashamedly open.

> And it came about that when Solomon had finished praying this entire prayer and supplication to the Lord, he arose from before the altar of the Lord, from kneeling on his knees with his hands spread toward heaven. And he stood and blessed all the assembly of Israel with a loud voice, saying, "Blessed be the Lord, who has given rest to His people Israel, according to all that He promised; not one word has failed of all His good promise, which He promised through Moses His servant. May the Lord our God be with us, as He was with our fathers; may He

not leave us or forsake us, that He may incline our hearts to Himself, to walk in all His ways and to keep His commandments and His statutes and His ordinances, which He commanded our fathers. And may these words of mine, with which I have made supplication before the Lord, be near to the Lord our God day and night, that He may maintain the cause of His servant and the cause of His people Israel, as each day requires, so that all the peoples of the earth may know that the Lord is God; there is no one else. Let your heart therefore be wholly devoted to the Lord our God, to walk in His statutes and to keep His commandments, as at this day." (8:54–61)

Humility. Integrity. Loyalty. If we were to typecast Solomon, these are the qualities we should focus on.

II. Solomon—Author and Composer

Solomon was a Renaissance man in every sense of the word—his interests were broad; his intelligence, deep.

> Now God gave Solomon wisdom and very great discernment and breadth of mind, like the sand that is on the seashore. And Solomon's wisdom surpassed the wisdom of all the sons of the east and all the wisdom of Egypt. For he was wiser than all men, than Ethan the Ezrahite, Heman, Calcol and Darda, the sons of Mahol; and his fame was known in all the surrounding nations. He also spoke 3,000 proverbs, and his songs were 1,005. And he spoke of trees, from the cedar that is in Lebanon even to the hyssop that grows on the wall; he spoke also of animals and birds and creeping things and fish. And men came from all peoples to hear the wisdom of Solomon, from all the kings of the earth who had heard of his wisdom. (1 Kings 4:29–34)

His interests included writing, music, botany, and various branches of zoology. His peers included Ethan the Ezrahite, Heman, and Calcol and Darda, who were the sons of Mahol. Faceless names to us today, but these were the Einsteins ... the Nobel Prize winners ... the Pulitzer Prize winners ... the intellectual elite of that day. In Solomon, we find authentic spirituality wedded to academic excellence. These qualities give birth to an appreciation for beauty, diversity, and creativity.

┌─ *Learning from Solomon* ─────────────────────

In his award-winning book *Addicted to Mediocrity,* Franky Schaeffer comments:

> If from this world around us we can learn anything about God's character, surely it is that we

have a creative God, a God of diversity, a God whose interest in beauty and detail must be unquestioned when one looks at the world which he has made around us, and people themselves as the result of his craftsmanship.

We could live in a flat uninteresting world, one that had the bare minimum of gray ingredients to support life, one whose diversity was only enough to provide the minimum of existence. Instead, we live in a riotous explosion of diversity and beauty. We live in a world full of "useless" beauty, we live in a world of millions of species, we live in a world peopled by individuals of infinite variety, talents, abilities, and this is only on our own planet. When one looks heavenward and sees the complexity of the reaches of space above us, the mind boggles at the creativity of our God.[1]

III. Solomon—Administrator and Architect

Not only was Solomon a man of God, an artist, and a scholar—he was a skilled administrator as well. Chapter 4 of 1 Kings reveals his herculean task: "Now King Solomon was king over all Israel" (v. 1). As a gifted administrator, Solomon divided his many responsibilities into manageable pieces, delegating the tasks to capable men. Verses 2–6 list Solomon's officials, while verses 7–19 list his twelve deputies.[2] Solomon's administrative gifts were also utilized in the architectural realm. His projects included houses, reservoirs, gardens, orchards, and vineyards (Eccles. 2:4–6). However, the most noted jewel in his architectural crown was the temple he built for the Lord (1 Kings 6).[3] The project was not massive, at least in size. The temple was only ninety feet long, thirty feet wide, and forty-five feet high (v. 2). But in scope, the task took a marathon seven and a half years to complete (vv. 37–38). Though unimpressive in size, the craftsmanship was exceedingly elaborate. A porch led into the main sanctuary (v. 3), and "for the house he made windows with artistic

---

1. Franky Schaeffer, *Addicted to Mediocrity: 20th Century Christians and the Arts* (Westchester, Ill.: Crossway Books, 1981), p. 17.

2. Other examples of Solomon's administrative abilities can be found in 1 Kings 5:14–18 and 9:17–23.

3. For a detailed description, consult *The Zondervan Pictorial Encyclopedia of the Bible,* Merrill C. Tenney, gen. ed. (Grand Rapids, Mich.: Zondervan Publishing House, 1976), vol. 5, p. 472.

frames" (v. 4). For Solomon, form was as important as function; beauty, as important as utility. The doors were not simply made to open and close; they were adorned with intricate carvings of cherubim, gourds, palm trees, and open flowers (vv. 18 and 32). The attention paid to artistic detail was time-consuming, as was the method of construction.

> And the house, while it was being built, was built of stone
> prepared at the quarry, and there was neither hammer
> nor axe nor any iron tool heard in the house while it was
> being built. (v. 7)

An unhurried but serious reverence paced the workers and permeated the atmosphere on the construction site. Gold was used to cover the entire temple as a symbol of the value of worship and fellowship with God.

> So Solomon overlaid the inside of the house with pure
> gold. And he drew chains of gold across the front of the
> inner sanctuary; and he overlaid it with gold. And he
> overlaid the whole house with gold, until all the house
> was finished. Also the whole altar which was by the inner
> sanctuary he overlaid with gold. (vv. 21–22)

Building according to Code

Solomon's temple was an architectural triumph of beauty and utility. Since it was the *sanctuary* of God—the place where God dwelt—only the best materials and artisans were accepted for the project. Technically, God does not dwell among men today in the same way He did during the Old Testament times. Instead, under the New Covenant, "*we* are the temple of the living God" (2 Cor. 6:16b, emphasis added).

> According to the grace of God which was given to
> me, as a wise master builder I laid a foundation,
> and another is building upon it. But let each man
> be careful how he builds upon it. For no man can
> lay a foundation other than the one which is laid,
> which is Jesus Christ. Now if any man builds upon
> the foundation with gold, silver, precious stones,
> wood, hay, straw, each man's work will become
> evident; for the day will show it, because it is to be
> revealed with fire; and the fire itself will test the
> quality of each man's work. If any man's work
> which he has built upon it remains, he shall receive
> a reward. If any man's work is burned up, he shall
> suffer loss; but he himself shall be saved, yet so as
> through fire. Do you not know that you are a temple

of God, and that the Spirit of God dwells in you? If
any man destroys the temple of God, God will
destroy him, for the temple of God is holy, and that
is what you are. (1 Cor. 3:10–17)

Take a look at your spiritual temple. Foundation a little shaky?
Rafters sagging? Gold turning a telltale green? Are you working
with a good contractor—"a wise master builder"—or are you
going the do-it-yourself route? Are you using gold, silver, and
precious stones—or are you trying to get by with economy-
grade wood, hay, and straw? You are the *temple* of the living
God and your spiritual life is no place to cut corners . . . is it?

IV. Solomon—Diplomat and Businessman

We have seen Solomon as an authentic man of God, author, academi-
cian, administrator, and architect. Now we will observe him in arenas
ranging from making allies to making horse trades.

   A. **Making allies** (1 Kings 5:1–18, 9:26–28). Like all leaders,
   Solomon occasionally treaded upon the thin ice of creating and
   maintaining alliances. One alliance was with Hiram.

   Now Hiram king of Tyre sent his servants to Solomon,
   when he heard that they had anointed him king in
   place of his father, for Hiram had always been a friend
   of David. (v. 1)

   When Solomon came to the throne, his relationship with Hiram
   was uncertain, because Hiram didn't know whether the new king
   would maintain his father's alliances. Solomon, however, wisely
   worked out a business transaction that would put the relationship on solid footing.

   So Hiram gave Solomon as much as he desired of the
   cedar and cypress timber. Solomon then gave Hiram
   20,000 kors of wheat as food for his household, and
   twenty kors of beaten oil; thus Solomon would give
   Hiram year by year. And the Lord gave wisdom to
   Solomon, just as He promised him; and there was
   peace between Hiram and Solomon, and the two of
   them made a covenant. (vv. 10–12)

   B. **Making trades** (1 Kings 4:26, 10:26–29; 2 Chron. 9:28).
   Solomon's interests in horses extended as far as Egypt in procur-
   ing the best for his chariots and horsemen. In all, he had forty
   thousand stalls of horses, fourteen hundred chariots, and twelve
   thousand horsemen. Again, in choosing the best animals and in
   making the best deals, insightful wisdom was paramount.

Emulating Solomon

As we wrap up this thumbnail sketch of Solomon, we see that he was indeed a multi-talented, live-life-to-the-hilt type of person. He used the gifts God had given him to the fullest ... and by doing so, gave glory to God. The exhortation of this lesson is to emulate Solomon. We conclude our study with an encouraging word of exhortation from Franky Schaeffer.

> "The world had many kings," said his contemporary Aretino, "but only one Michelangelo." ...
>
> By expressing yourself as an artist and by exercising those talents God has given you, you are praising him. Whether what you express is "religious" or "secular," as a Christian you are praising him. Everything is his....
>
> Remember that as a creative person, the important thing is to create. Who sees what you make, where it goes and what it does is a secondary consideration; the first is to exercise the talent God has given you.[4]

 Living Insights

Study One

From the historical accounts we have seen that Solomon was gifted in a wide variety of areas. Let's examine some of Solomon's personal writings to understand his feelings regarding several of these gifts.

- In Proverbs 3:1–12, Solomon talks about a right relationship with God. This passage mentions at least seven benefits. What are they?
- Solomon was known for his incredible wisdom. In Proverbs 3:13–20, wisdom's value is shown in ten different ways. Write them down and think of ways to apply them to your life.
- As an effective administrator, Solomon had the proper perspective on work, riches, and rewards. From Ecclesiastes 5:8–20 answer the following:
  —What is frustrating about work?
  —What is the right attitude toward riches?
  —How does God fit into all of this?

---

4. Schaeffer, *Addicted to Mediocrity,* pp. 59–60.

Living Insights

Are you able to relate to what's happening in the life of Solomon? Let's continue our look at his life by interacting with the following questions. Be open, honest, and allow God to speak to you.

- Solomon: man of God, author, composer, architect, administrator, diplomat, businessman ... he was quite diversified. How about you? What should follow your name? Think hard and try to come up with a few descriptions.

- Is there more you'd like to accomplish in life? Look up James 4:13–15 and answer this question based on verse 15: What is the "'this or that'" in your life? List your most important goals.

- Let's spend some time in prayer. Solomon was known for his godliness. Are you? Ask God to develop this quality in you.

Signs of Erosion
Selected Scripture

The Colorado River serpentines through the Arizona desert taking little snaky licks along its path. It twists and turns, winding its way through sandstone, limestone, shale, and granite, biting chunks out of the banks. Tirelessly—day in, day out—the reptilian river slithers its way through the earth's strata. Writhing, laden with silt, the underbelly of the relentless river wears away the rock . . . grain by grain . . . pebble by pebble . . . day by day . . . year by year. The result? The Grand Canyon. More than half a million tons of sediment are eroded each day from the canyon. Though the river is the main erosive agent in the canyon, it is by no means the *only* agent. Water flowing from short, violent rainstorms pushes sediment down slopes where there is little vegetation to impede it. Roots of trees and other plants burrowing into cracks pry the rocks loose, sending them crashing into the hungry river below. The chemical action of lichens eats away at the rocks they cling to. Water hiding in the hairline fissures of giant boulders freezes in the winter and chips away at their stony surfaces. Even the wind, with its blasts of airborn sand, pits away at the huge, gaping void of the canyon. It's a monument now—that gash across the face of Arizona—a jagged testimony to the sweeping, destructive power of erosion. Character can erode like that, a grain of sand at a time . . . even character of granite, as polished as Solomon's.

I. A Flawless Image

Solomon stood exalted in the world as a towering, sculpted monument. There was no one as great, as wise, as rich, as envied.

A. The blessing of God (2 Chron. 1:1–12, 1 Kings 3:13). As it was Michelangelo's touch that turned a block of stone into the exalted *Pietà,* so it was the touch of God that carved Solomon's place in history.

> Now Solomon the son of David established himself securely over his kingdom, and the Lord his God was with him and exalted him greatly. And Solomon spoke to all Israel, to the commanders of thousands and of hundreds and to the judges and to every leader in all Israel, the heads of the fathers' households. Then Solomon, and all the assembly with him, went to the high place which was at Gibeon; for God's tent of meeting was there, which Moses the servant of the Lord had made in the wilderness. However, David had brought up the ark of God from Kiriath-jearim to the place he had prepared for it; for he had pitched a tent for it in Jerusalem. Now the bronze altar, which Bezalel the son of Uri, the son of Hur, had made, was there before the tabernacle of

the Lord, and Solomon and the assembly sought it out. And Solomon went up there before the Lord to the bronze altar which was at the tent of meeting, and offered a thousand burnt offerings on it. In that night God appeared to Solomon and said to him, "Ask what I shall give you." (2 Chron. 1:1–7)

So great was God's faith in Solomon that He gave him a blank-check opportunity to ask for *whatever* he wanted.

And Solomon said to God, "Thou hast dealt with my father David with great lovingkindness, and hast made me king in his place. Now, O Lord God, Thy promise to my father David is fulfilled; for Thou hast made me king over a people as numerous as the dust of the earth. Give me now wisdom and knowledge, that I may go out and come in before this people; for who can rule this great people of Thine?" (vv. 8–10)

Because of the purity of Solomon's request—wisdom to rule God's people—God gave "exceeding abundantly beyond all" that he asked or imagined (Eph. 3:20).

And God said to Solomon, "Because you had this in mind, and did not ask for riches, wealth, or honor, or the life of those who hate you, nor have you even asked for long life, but you have asked for yourself wisdom and knowledge, that you may rule My people, over whom I have made you king, wisdom and knowledge have been granted to you. And I will give you riches and wealth and honor, such as none of the kings who were before you has possessed, nor those who will come after you." (vv. 11–12)

Solomon would be so blessed that he would be without a peer: "There will not be any among the kings like you all your days" (1 Kings 3:13b).

B. A variety of interests (1 Kings 4:29–34). Like the glistening, snowcapped peak of Mount Everest, Solomon was the pinnacle of God's blessing on earth. His horizons of interest, as we have studied, were limitless—like the view from Everest. Therefore, when he fell, it was from great heights and over a wide territory.

C. A record of achievements (1 Kings 6:1, 38, 7:1; Eccles. 2:4–6). In an unparalleled operation of cosmetic surgery, Solomon reconstructed the sagging face of Israel. For a duration of at least twenty years, Solomon smoothed the country's architectural wrinkles. Pools, houses, resorts, stables, fortresses, an exquisite home, and the breathtaking temple stood as tributes not only to his architectural and administrative skill but to his surgeon's patience as well.

D. The praise of men (1 Kings 10:1, 6, 23–24). A regular parade of fans pilgrimaged from the corners of the world to behold Solomon and all his glory. Like groupies, they gathered around his throne to pay him tribute, to pick his brain on difficult issues, to gather the pearls of wisdom that cascaded so fluidly from his lips. Fortune, fame, friends, and fulfilled fantasies became his daily delights. But like a steady diet of luscious desserts, these pleasures soon sated his appetite and made him nauseous.

What Is It That Really Lasts?

Solomon's glory soon began to lose its luster. Earthly pleasures have a way of doing that, as the poet Robert Burns noted:

> But pleasures are like poppies spread:
> You seize the flower, its bloom is shed;
> Or like the snow falls in the river:
> A moment white—then melts forever.[1]

Then what *does* last?

> All flesh is grass, and all its loveliness is like
>   the flower of the field.
> The grass withers, the flower fades,
> But the word of our God stands forever.
> (Isa. 40:6b, 8)

His Word is what lasts. Are you investing enough of your time in it? Enough of your life? A lot of what busies us will eventually fade and melt away. Only His Word *really* lasts. Only His Word keeps our characters from eroding (Ps. 119:9, 11).

II. A Subtle Trap (Ecclesiastes 2)

In Solomon's diary—Ecclesiastes—the king's words float off the page bloated and bilious from an overfed ego. The words *I* and *for myself* are dished up throughout the passage like second, third, fourth, and fifth helpings, until he finally becomes fed up with it all and pushes the plate away.

> I said to myself, "Come now, I will test you with pleasure. So enjoy yourself." And behold, it too was futility. I said of laughter, "It is madness," and of pleasure, "What does it accomplish?" I explored with my mind how to stimulate my body with wine while my mind was guiding me wisely, and how to take hold of folly, until I could see

1. Burton Stevenson, *The Home Book of Quotations; Classical and Modern,* 10th ed. (1967; reprint, New York, N.Y.: Dodd, Mead and Co., 1984), p. 1512.

what good there is for the sons of men to do under heaven the few years of their lives. I enlarged my works: I built houses for myself, I planted vineyards for myself; I made gardens and parks for myself, and I planted in them all kinds of fruit trees; I made ponds of water for myself from which to irrigate a forest of growing trees. I bought male and female slaves, and I had homeborn slaves. Also I possessed flocks and herds larger than all who preceded me in Jerusalem. Also, I collected for myself silver and gold, and the treasure of kings and provinces. I provided for myself male and female singers and the pleasures of men—many concubines. Then I became great and increased more than all who preceded me in Jerusalem. My wisdom also stood by me. And all that my eyes desired I did not refuse them. I did not withhold my heart from any pleasure, for my heart was pleased because of all my labor and this was my reward for all my labor. Thus I considered all my activities which my hands had done and the labor which I had exerted, and behold all was vanity and striving after wind and there was no profit under the sun. (Eccles. 2:1–11)

Alka-Seltzer for the Soul

Bored and disillusioned, nothing satisfied Solomon any longer; nothing stimulated him. His taste buds had had it! He was stuffed, nauseated. So full of himself, so full of life's pleasures, he was ready to throw up. But that all-you-can-eat buffet life-style also seems to be the diet of most Americans. Eventually it leads to heartburn.

> Americans have always been able to handle auster-ity and even adversity. Prosperity is what's doing us in.[2]

Need a little relief from the heartburn of living for yourself? If so, try a change in your eating habits—for " ' "Man shall not live on bread alone, but on every word that proceeds out of the mouth of God" ' " (Matt. 4:4).

III. A Deteriorating Life

From a distance, Solomon's exquisitely hewn character looms impressive and striking. But a closer look reveals signs of erosion: a chip here . . . a crack there . . . a compromise here . . . a crumbling conviction there. However polished his granite character, Solomon—

2. James Reston in *3,500 Good Quotes for Speakers,* p. 194.

17

like all of us—had feet of clay. And those feet of clay were slowly beginning to wash out beneath him. Very few things deteriorate *suddenly*. No church suddenly splits. No child suddenly becomes delinquent. No friendship suddenly ends. No marriage suddenly dissolves. No building suddenly collapses. No Grand Canyon suddenly forms. It happens *slowly* . . . grain by grain . . . compromise by compromise. If you see erosion taking place in your life, it's time to start a soul conservation project and repair the foundations of your relationship with the Lord.

> "Therefore everyone who hears these words of Mine, and acts upon them, may be compared to a wise man, who built his house upon the rock. And the rain descended, and the floods came, and the winds blew, and burst against that house; and yet it did not fall, for it had been founded upon the rock. And everyone who hears these words of Mine, and does not act upon them, will be like a foolish man, who built his house upon the sand. And the rain descended, and the floods came, and the winds blew, and burst against that house; and it fell, and great was its fall." (Matt. 7:24–27)

If the erosion isn't stopped, the rains of life's storms will wash you away.

A. Unwise alliances with unbelievers (1 Kings 3:1; 7:8; 9:16, 24). The first sign of erosion we see in Solomon's character is a little chip of compromise.

> Then Solomon formed a marriage alliance with Pharaoh king of Egypt, and took Pharaoh's daughter and brought her to the city of David, until he had finished building his own house and the house of the Lord and the wall around Jerusalem. (1 Kings 3:1)

Solomon's marriage with Pharaoh's daughter was a union of two nations—not of two people. It was a marriage of expedience—not obedience to God's precepts. It was based on political diplomacy—not love. Furthermore, it was a compromise of God's Word. In Deuteronomy 7:1–11, God lays down some very specific instructions to Israel regarding intermarriage with foreigners who worshiped other gods (see also Exod. 23:31–32, 34:12–16, and Ezra 9:2). Although we do see some conviction from Solomon on the matter (2 Chron. 8:11), his grip on God's Word shows definite signs of loosening.

An Afterthought on Alliances

An unequal yoke (2 Cor. 6:14) will distribute the burden of the relationship unevenly. At best, you can expect blistered

---

> shoulders. At worst, you can be pulled off a path of obedience and fall, crippled, into a ditch.

B. **Unresolved conflicts with friends** (1 Kings 9:10–14). In a business transaction with his friend Hiram, Solomon traded several cities in exchange for building materials. Hiram later inspected his newly acquired real estate and found he'd been cheated.

> And it came about at the end of twenty years in which Solomon had built the two houses, the house of the Lord and the king's house (Hiram king of Tyre had supplied Solomon with cedar and cypress timber and gold according to all his desire), then King Solomon gave Hiram twenty cities in the land of Galilee. So Hiram came out from Tyre to see the cities which Solomon had given him, and they did not please him. And he said, "What are these cities which you have given me, my brother?" So they were called the land of Cabul[3] to this day.

Although he had been slighted, Hiram attempted to reconcile matters with Solomon (v. 14). However, Solomon made no effort to admit the wrong or to make things right. Again, we see signs of Solomon's character eroding in a shady business deal and ill-treatment of a friend.

C. **Unrestrained preoccupation with sex** (1 Kings 11:1–8). Solomon not only had Pharaoh's daughter as a wife, he indulged himself in a harem that was unequaled in the ancient Near East. It was his unrestrained preoccupation with sex that ultimately led him away from God.

> Now King Solomon loved many foreign women along with the daughter of Pharaoh: Moabite, Ammonite, Edomite, Sidonian, and Hittite women, from the nations concerning which the Lord had said to the sons of Israel, "You shall not associate with them, neither shall they associate with you, for they will surely turn your heart away after their gods." Solomon held fast to these in love. And he had seven hundred wives, princesses, and three hundred concubines, and his wives turned his heart away. (vv. 1–3)

Again, Solomon turned his head away from the clear teaching of God's Word (Deut. 7:3–4). As a result, his seductive wives

---

3. *Cabul* means "as good as nothing."

adulterated his heart.[4] As he let sin creep in, little by little, Solomon's granite character began to erode away.

D. Unholy involvement with idolatry (1 Kings 11:4–8). With the introduction of more foreign wives, a spirit of religious infidelity infiltrated the nation.

> For it came about when Solomon was old, his wives turned his heart away after other gods; and his heart was not wholly devoted to the Lord his God, as the heart of David his father had been. For Solomon went after Ashtoreth the goddess of the Sidonians and after Milcom the detestable idol of the Ammonites. And Solomon did what was evil in the sight of the Lord, and did not follow the Lord fully, as David his father had done. Then Solomon built a high place for Chemosh the detestable idol of Moab, on the mountain which is east of Jerusalem, and for Molech the detestable idol of the sons of Ammon. Thus also he did for all his foreign wives, who burned incense and sacrificed to their gods.

The pagan altars of sacrifice, known as "high places," were still operational in spite of God's command to "'tear down their altars, and smash their sacred pillars, and hew down their Asherim, and burn their graven images with fire'" (Deut. 7:5). God's Word was slipping further out of Solomon's hand as his commitment to God slowly relaxed. Flirting with idolatry was beginning to open the floodgates of an erosive stream that would eventually wash away the clay feet of Solomon's character.

 Living Insights

Study One ━━━━━━━━━━━━━━━━━━━━━━━━━━━━━━━━━

Ecclesiastes 2 and 1 Corinthians 10 speak on the subtle trap of erosion. Paraphrase the following passages, and personalize them. Then, answer the following questions.

- Ecclesiastes 2:9–11: Why was extravagance unsatisfactory?
- Ecclesiastes 2:16–19: How does this relate to boredom and lack of stimulation?
- Ecclesiastes 2:20–24: What are some signs of disillusionment according to this passage?
- 1 Corinthians 10:11–12: How does this apply to you?

---

4. In the Old Testament, idolatry is viewed as spiritual prostitution and adultery (Jer. 2:20–28, 3:6–9). Anything we give our hearts to that competes with our relationship to God and causes us to be unfaithful to Him is a form of idolatry.

 *Living Insights*

Let's use this time to perform a personal examination of our lives. Deterioration is never sudden. It's the little things that cause erosion and ultimate decay. Ponder these questions, and write down honest answers.

- How would I handle immense wealth?
- How do I respond to boredom?
- To whom or what do I turn when disillusioned?
- In which one of these areas am I most susceptible?
    —unwise alliances with unbelievers
    —unresolved conflicts with friends
    —unrestrained preoccupation with sex
    —unholy involvement with idolatry
- How am I especially susceptible in this area?
- How can I defend myself from erosion in this area?
- Am I ignoring biblical counsel or applying it? In what area?
- Am I personally accountable? To whom? In what areas am I unaccountable?
- Discuss this list of questions with someone you are accountable to. Ask for an honest evaluation of these areas in your life.

When the Heart Is Turned Away
1 Kings 11:1–13

It doesn't take much to wreck a brand new automobile, whether it's a Volkswagen or a Rolls Royce. Too much to drink . . . too much daydreaming . . . too much nodding off at the wheel. Self-indulgence at the wrong times or in the wrong amounts can lead to disaster, whether that relates to driving a car or directing a kingdom. Cruising behind the wheel of a head-turning kingdom, Solomon had a heavy foot on the accelerator. Intoxicated with fame, fortune, and females, his spiritual eyelids were heavy with lethargy. It would take more than black coffee to sober him up to his responsibilities as ruler of God's people. With only one arm propped on the steering wheel of the kingdom, Solomon was fast on his way to becoming a spiritual fatality.

I. Analysis of Tangible Success
Like a teenager on a Friday night date in his father's new sports car, Solomon appeared to have it all. He had an incredible fortune (1 Kings 10:14–25), widespread fame (vv. 23–25), unlimited power (4:21–25), and innumerable pleasures (Eccles. 2:1–10). Although a young ruler in the driver's seat of a powerful kingdom, Solomon had been given the keys with both God's and his father's blessing (1 Chron. 28:5). And in that driver's seat, he sat tall and proud and "became greater than all the kings of the earth in riches and in wisdom" (1 Kings 10:23). Here was a young man who literally had it all: he was born with a silver spoon in his mouth, had the blessing of God, a marvelous heritage, good training at the feet of Nathan the prophet, a father who would be the envy of any son, *and* . . . a heart that beat strong and sincere for God. So what, then, broke down? What came loose? What went out of alignment?

II. Characteristics of Personal Deterioration
The problem in Solomon's life appears to have been a slow leak in his relationship with God. A pinprick leak, unattended, is all it took. Day by day a little spiritual air seeped out of Solomon's life, until one day he woke up and found his relationship with God flat.

A. Internal attitudes. Two sharp slivers slowly penetrated Solomon's relationship with God: failing to take God seriously and failing to be accountable.

1. **Failing to take God seriously.** Solomon tolerated what God condemned and embraced what God abhorred. Doing so, he failed to take God at His word.

> Then Solomon formed a marriage alliance with Pharaoh king of Egypt, and took Pharaoh's daughter and brought her to the city of David, until he had finished building his own house and the

> house of the Lord and the wall around Jerusalem.
> The people were still sacrificing on the high
> places, because there was no house built for the
> name of the Lord until those days. Now Solomon
> loved the Lord, walking in the statutes of his
> father David, except he sacrificed and burned
> incense on the high places. (1 Kings 3:1–3)

Throughout the writings of Moses, God warns against this
practice of marrying foreign women. But Solomon doesn't
take it seriously. In the parallel book of 2 Chronicles, we see
more visible evidence of Solomon's sagging spiritual attitudes.

> Then Solomon brought Pharaoh's daughter up
> from the city of David to the house which he had
> built for her; for he said, "My wife shall not dwell
> in the house of David king of Israel, because the
> places are holy where the ark of the Lord has
> entered." (8:11)

Apparently, Solomon had brought his Egyptian wife to the
city of David and kept her there under wraps ... hidden behind the scenes so as not to attract too much attention. To
Solomon's credit, we do see *some* conviction in his life. His
relationship with God was not totally flat yet. " 'My wife
shall not dwell in the house of David king of Israel, because
the places are holy where the ark of the Lord has entered' "
(v. 11b). Now look closely at the first half of the verse and
notice the sliver: "Then Solomon brought Pharaoh's daughter
up from the city of David to the house which he had built
for her" (v. 11a, emphasis added). Solomon knew that a
woman from an unholy background had no business being
in a holy place. But to his discredit, he found a place for
her *somewhere* in his kingdom, built a house for her, and
undoubtedly spent much time there himself. Having made
a place for her in his kingdom and in his heart, he opened
a Pandora's box of idolatry, infidelity, and innumerable
other iniquities.

Gauging Pressure

Like an overinflated tire, Solomon had many internal
pressures that made him more vulnerable to spiritual
blowout. First, he was *overexposed* to the things of
God—which led to cynicism. In his youth, Solomon
trafficked heavily in spiritual things. But he gradually
lost his sensitivity toward God, and calluses inevitably

resulted. Second, he was *overindulged,* given too much for nothing—which led to irresponsibility. David did the fighting while Solomon received the benefits. Third, he was *overpromoted,* pushed too far up too fast—which led to sterile professionalism. Solomon missed many of the growing pains and pleasures of the upward climb on the professional ladder. With Solomon's folly in mind, give your life a quick three-point check. Have you been overexposed? Overindulged? Overpromoted? Are you doing this to your children . . . the people you work with . . . the church? Remember: *Overinflated tires wear out faster and are more susceptible to blowouts.*

2. **Failing to be accountable.** Solomon was alone in the driver's seat of the kingdom. He was accountable to no one. He answered to no one. The words "all that Solomon desired to do" (1 Kings 9:1b) and "all that it pleased Solomon to build" (v. 19b, 2 Chron. 8:6b) reflected the absolute nature of his rule. He acquired vast riches and constructed sprawling storage cities to secure them. He also built elaborate centers for his horses, horsemen, and chariots.

> So Solomon rebuilt Gezer and the lower Beth-horon and Baalath and Tamar in the wilderness, in the land of Judah, and all the storage cities which Solomon had, even the cities for his chariots and the cities for his horsemen, and all that it pleased Solomon to build in Jerusalem, in Lebanon, and in all the land under his rule.
> (1 Kings 9:17–19)

Whatever "pleased Solomon" he did. Whatever he desired, longed for, coveted was his. This unaccountability was passed on to his son Rehoboam, who ruled according to his capricious desires and "forsook the counsel of the elders" (2 Chron. 10:6–8).

Biblical Accountability

The New Testament shows us the refined sense of accountability we ought to have toward one another. Children should be accountable to parents; wives, to husbands; husbands, to Christ; laypeople, to elders; citizens, to government; one, to another, and so forth. The key to *all* these relationships is submission—servanthood that flows out of humility, honor, and love for one another. Husbands are directed to love

---

their wives in a sacrificial and sensitive way (Eph. 5:25, 1 Pet. 3:7), fathers are to deal tenderly with their children (Eph. 6:4), and elders are commissioned to be shepherds of their flock, not lords (1 Pet. 5:1–3). How sensitive, servantlike, shepherdlike, and sacrificial are you to those who are accountable *to you?* How accountable are you *to others?*

B. External action. God visited Solomon on three specific occasions.

   1. **The first encounter was at his inauguration to the throne** (1 Kings 3:5–14). Their meeting was one of the most beautiful in all the Scriptures. God told Solomon in a dream: " 'Ask what you wish me to give you' " (v. 5). Solomon responded with a purely motivated request for " 'an understanding heart to judge Thy people to discern between good and evil' " (v. 9). In verses 12–14 God grants the wish and adds a postscripted promise.

   > "Behold, I have done according to your words. Behold, I have given you a wise and discerning heart, so that there has been no one like you before you, nor shall one like you arise after you. And I have also given you what you have not asked, both riches and honor, so that there will not be any among the kings like you all your days. And if you walk in My ways, keeping My statutes and commandments, as your father David walked, then I will prolong your days."

   2. **The second encounter is found in 1 Kings 9:1–9.** This time, however, a tone of caution tinges God's words.

   > "And as for you, if you will walk before Me as your father David walked, in integrity of heart and uprightness, doing according to all that I have commanded you and will keep My statutes and My ordinances, then I will establish the throne of your kingdom over Israel forever, just as I promised to your father David, saying, 'You shall not lack a man on the throne of Israel.' But if you or your sons shall indeed turn away from following Me, and shall not keep My commandments and My statutes which I have set before you and shall go and serve other gods and worship them, then I will cut off Israel from the land which I have given them, and the house which I have

consecrated for My name, I will cast out of My sight. So Israel will become a proverb and a byword among all peoples. And this house will become a heap of ruins; everyone who passes by will be astonished and hiss and say, 'Why has the Lord done thus to this land and to this house?' And they will say, 'Because they forsook the Lord their God, who brought their fathers out of the land of Egypt, and adopted other gods and worshiped them and served them, therefore the Lord has brought all this adversity on them.' " (vv. 4–9)

God sees the leak in Solomon's life and is cautioning him to patch it before he destroys the kingdom.

3. The third encounter occurs in 1 Kings 11. This time, the tone is castigatory. God is angry—and for good reason. Power had corrupted the pure heart of the throne.

Unaccountable Authority

"Power tends to corrupt and absolute power corrupts absolutely."[1] Solomon was a pure and wise man at the inception of his rule. But no man is good enough or wise enough to be trusted with unlimited power. Power is heady wine that will intoxicate the best of hearts, dull the best of minds, and blur the best of vision. History is replete with the strewn wreckage of empires driven over the cliffs by rulers made dizzy with the strong drink of unaccountable authority. And, sadly, Solomon was no exception.

III. Final Steps of Failure

The backdrop to God's anger in 1 Kings 11 is found in Deuteronomy 17:14–17, where the job description for Israel's kings is on file.

"When you enter the land which the Lord your God gives you, and you possess it and live in it, and you say, 'I will set a king over me like all the nations who are around me,' you shall surely set a king over you whom the Lord your God chooses, one from among your countrymen you shall set as king over yourselves; you may not put a foreigner over yourselves who is not your countryman. Moreover, he shall not multiply horses for himself, nor

---

1. Lord Acton in *Bartlett's Familiar Quotations,* 14th ed., Emily Morison Beck, ed. (Boston, Mass.: Little, Brown and Co., 1968), p. 750.

26

shall he cause the people to return to Egypt to multiply horses, since the Lord has said to you, 'You shall never again return that way.' Neither shall he multiply wives for himself, lest his heart turn away; nor shall he greatly increase silver and gold for himself."

In the course of his lengthy reign, Solomon violated almost every one of God's stipulations: he not only multiplied horses for himself, but he went as far as Egypt to acquire them; he multiplied wives for himself, as well as gold and silver. Turning now to 1 Kings 11, we see the bellows that inflamed God's wrath. In verse 1, Solomon willingly ignored God's written Word by marrying foreign women. In verse 2, he arrogantly flaunted his desires by holding "fast to these [wives] in love." In verses 4 and 6, we see these same wives entice his now divided heart to spiritual adultery. Finally, in verses 5–8 we see the specific graven images that were the objects of Solomon's idolatry.

For Solomon went after Ashtoreth the goddess of the Sidonians and after Milcom the detestable idol of the Ammonites. And Solomon did what was evil in the sight of the Lord, and did not follow the Lord fully, as David his father had done. Then Solomon built a high place for Chemosh the detestable idol of Moab, on the mountain which is east of Jerusalem, and for Molech the detestable idol of the sons of Ammon. Thus also he did for all his foreign wives, who burned incense and sacrificed to their gods. (vv. 5–8)[2]

In the verses that follow, we feel the heat and see the flame in God's eyes as He speaks to Solomon.

Now the Lord was angry with Solomon because his heart was turned away from the Lord, the God of Israel, who had appeared to him twice, and had commanded him concerning this thing, that he should not go after other gods; but he did not observe what the Lord had commanded. So the Lord said to Solomon, "Because you have done this, and you have not kept My covenant and My statutes, which I have commanded you, I will surely tear the kingdom from you, and will give it to your servant." (vv. 9–11)

A Concluding Application

First Kings 11 reads like a tragic accident report of a drunken driver. Too much indulgence. Too little resistance. Too much

---

2. Ashtoreth was the goddess of love, maternity, and fertility. Milcom was the Ammonite god of authority. Chemosh and Molech were gods whose rituals included child sacrifice.

power. Too little restraint. At first, the joyride is filled with thrills and laughter. But notice how Solomon's tires gradually drift into the oncoming lane: "Now King Solomon loved many foreign women" (v. 1) . . . "and his wives turned his heart away" (v. 3) . . . "his wives turned his heart away after other gods; and his heart was not wholly devoted to the Lord his God, as the heart of David his father had been" (v. 4) . . . "and Solomon did what was evil in the sight of the Lord" (v. 6). In a drunken stupor of self-indulgence, Solomon skids around the hairpin turns of promiscuity and idolatry, speeding with his headlights off. As a result, God does what any good friend would do: He grabs the steering wheel, hits the brakes, and takes away the keys (v. 11). Let me conclude by talking to you briefly, as a friend. Are the tires of your life drifting into some wrong lanes? Are you beginning to skid into the oncoming traffic of God's judgment? If so, please, *please* pull over. Put yourself in the hands of someone who cares, and let that friend drive you home, back to Jesus, where you belong—before you become another grim highway statistic.

 Living Insights

Study One

Solomon's reckless life bottoms out in 1 Kings 11:1–13. This passage is worthy of further study. Using the chart below as a suggested format, record on a sheet of paper as many observations as you can find within these four categories. (Example: Solomon loved many foreign women, v. 1.)

Solomon		His Wives		The Lord God		Foreign Gods	
Observations	Verses	Observations	Verses	Observations	Verses	Observations	Verses

- Based on this lesson and your observations from this study, put into your own words the reasons Solomon fell. How do they relate to you? What could cause you to fall?

Living Insights

Turning a heart away from God is a serious matter . . . one worth much study and reflection. Copy this chart on a separate piece of paper. Ten statements are drawn from this lesson and are placed in the left-hand column. In the center column, restate the concept in your own words. Then, under the heading "Plans," jot down several ways to take positive action for eliminating erosion in your life.

Principles	Paraphrases	Plans
1. Solomon did not take God seriously.		
2. Overexposure to the things of God leads to cynicism.		
3. Indulgence leads to irresponsibility.		
4. Quick promotion leads to sterile professionalism.		
5. Solomon was not accountable to any person.		
6. Solomon willfully ignored God's Word.		
7. Solomon flaunted his own desires.		
8. Solomon resisted total commitment to God.		
9. Solomon pursued the companionship of the ungodly.		
10. No heart is suddenly turned away.		

How God Deals with Defiance

1 Kings 11:9–40

In the long season of his reign, Solomon sowed a lot of chaff to the wind, a lot of empty husks of self-indulgence. It is no wonder he came to the conclusion that so much of his life was vanity...emptiness...striving after the wind (Eccles. 2:10–11). It is also no surprise that Solomon would eventually harvest what he sowed. "For they sow the wind, / And they reap the whirlwind" (Hosea 8:7a). Solomon had sown the winds of wickedness, and on the horizon was the whirlwind of God's wrath. In the Old Testament, the image of the whirlwind is associated with God's judgment (Ps. 58:9, Prov. 10:25).

> A jealous and avenging God is the Lord;
> The Lord is avenging and wrathful.
> The Lord takes vengeance on His adversaries,
> And He reserves wrath for His enemies.
> The Lord is slow to anger and great in power,
> And the Lord will by no means leave the guilty unpunished.
> In whirlwind and storm is His way....(Nahum 1:2–3)

In 1 Kings 11 we see the storm of God's anger in a caldron of impending judgment, stirred by Solomon's involvement with idolatry (vv. 1–8). However, it is Solomon's *defiance* in the face of God's rebuke that causes the caldron to bubble over. Ironically, Solomon's own testimony about defiance returns later in his life to indict him.

> "Because I called, and you refused;
> I stretched out my hand, and no one paid attention;
> And you neglected all my counsel,
> And did not want my reproof;
> I will laugh at your calamity;
> I will mock when your dread comes,
> When your dread comes like a storm,
> And your calamity comes on like a whirlwind...."
> (Prov. 1:24–27)

I. Defiance: Seeds and Harvest

The wrath of God has spilled over onto mankind's wickedness since the Fall (see Gen. 3 and Rom. 1:18–21). As in Solomon's case, much of that wrath resulted from idolatry.

> Professing to be wise, they became fools, and exchanged the glory of the incorruptible God for an image in the form of corruptible man and of birds and four-footed animals and crawling creatures. Therefore God gave them over in the lusts of their hearts to impurity, that their bodies might be dishonored among them. For they exchanged the truth of God for a lie, and worshiped and served the

30

creature rather than the Creator, who is blessed forever. Amen. (Rom. 1:22–25)

But idolatry is only an outward manifestation of hearts in rebellion, of people in defiance: "slanderers, haters of God, insolent, arrogant, boastful, inventors of evil, disobedient to parents" (Rom. 1:30). In God's eyes, idolatry and rebellion are fruit and root of the same tree: " 'For rebellion is as the sin of divination, / And insubordination is as iniquity and idolatry' " (1 Sam. 15:23a). So dangerous is the character trait of defiance that extreme measures were instituted in Israel's legal system to protect the community from its malignant spread.

> "If any man has a stubborn and rebellious son who will not obey his father or his mother, and when they chastise him, he will not even listen to them, then his father and mother shall seize him, and bring him out to the elders of his city at the gateway of his home town. And they shall say to the elders of his city, 'This son of ours is stubborn and rebellious, he will not obey us, he is a glutton and a drunkard.' Then all the men of his city shall stone him to death; so you shall remove the evil from your midst, and all Israel shall hear of it and fear." (Deut. 21:18–21)

In 1 Kings 11 we find a stubborn, rebellious, defiant man; not a young man still living at home, as in Deuteronomy 21, but an adult of at least forty-five years of age. Not just any man, but the richest man in all the world—the son of David—king of Israel—Solomon. The seeds he threw to the wind were compromise, extravagance, unaccountability, and idolatry. His harvest was a loss of distinctive convictions, boredom and disillusionment, unchecked independence, lust and open defiance. Two times in 1 Kings 11 we are told that his heart was turned away from God (vv. 4, 9). Consequently, because Solomon would not turn to God, God turned to him—in anger.

II. Reaction: God and Solomon (1 Kings 11:9–40)

Because God is slow to anger and infinitely compassionate (Ps. 103:8), we could easily be lulled into believing that He is soft and tolerant of sin. But His wrath, when kindled, is a consuming fire (Ps. 90:7).[1]

A. Divine anger (1 Kings 11:9–13). His wrath kindling, God ignites the tinders of judgment for the defiant king.

> Now the Lord was angry with Solomon because his heart was turned away from the Lord, the God of Israel, who had appeared to him twice, and had commanded him concerning this thing, that he should

---

1. The word *charah,* translated "to burn with anger" or "to be kindled with anger," is used in various forms 139 times in the Old Testament. It emphasizes the kindling of anger, like the kindling of fire, or the heat of the anger once kindled. Compare Numbers 11:33, 12:9 and Psalms 69:24, 74:1.

not go after other gods; but he did not observe what the Lord had commanded. So the Lord said to Solomon, "Because you have done this, and you have not kept My covenant and My statutes, which I have commanded you, I will surely tear the kingdom from you, and will give it to your servant. Nevertheless I will not do it in your days for the sake of your father David, but I will tear it out of the hand of your son. However, I will not tear away all the kingdom, but I will give one tribe to your son for the sake of My servant David and for the sake of Jerusalem which I have chosen."

With the word *nevertheless* in verse 12, God's mercy pierced radiantly earthward through the ominous clouds of judgment that hovered on Israel's horizon. Because of His love for David and Jerusalem, God mercifully held back turbulent times of civil war until after Solomon's death.

Sunshine after the Storm

In the Scriptures, God's wrath is pictured as a cup from which we are sometimes made to drink (Jer. 25:15). By comparison, His lovingkindness is an everlasting well, quenching the thirst of generations (Ps. 136). God is slow to anger and abounding in lovingkindness (Neh. 9:17). But when He gets angry, we can take comfort that although weeping may last through the rainy night, the crisp break of a new day will follow, a pristine morning—sun shining radiantly, and warm with the grace of God.

> For His anger is but for a moment,
> His favor is for a lifetime. (Ps. 30:5a)

B. **Human adversaries** (1 Kings 11:14–25). Up until now Solomon had known only peace in his reign. But God, with His silent, sovereign whistle, was calling His hounds to begin nipping at the heels of Solomon's royal sandals.

> Then the Lord raised up an adversary to Solomon, Hadad the Edomite; he was of the royal line in Edom.... God also raised up another adversary to him, Rezon the son of Eliada, who had fled from his lord Hadadezer king of Zobah. (vv. 14, 23)

The first of Solomon's adversaries was Hadad the Edomite (vv. 14–22). Years before, this young prince narrowly managed to escape a massacre at the hands of David's army (vv. 15–17). He fled to Egypt, where he "found great favor before Pharaoh" (v. 19). Later, he married the Pharaoh's sister-in-law, who bore him a son (vv. 19–20). In the years that followed, however, neither the pleasures nor power of Pharaoh's palace could erase the scars Hadad had suffered from David.

> But when Hadad heard in Egypt that David slept with his fathers, and that Joab the commander of the army was dead, Hadad said to Pharaoh, "Send me away, that I may go to my own country." Then Pharaoh said to him, "But what have you lacked with me, that behold, you are seeking to go to your own country?" And he answered, "Nothing; nevertheless you must surely let me go." (vv. 21–22)

Clearly, Hadad was hot on the trail of revenge—a trail that led straight to David's heir, Solomon. Meanwhile, Rezon from Damascus, a wild dog from a different pack, was picking up Solomon's scent.

> And [Rezon] gathered men to himself and became leader of a marauding band, after David slew them of Zobah; and they went to Damascus and stayed there, and reigned in Damascus. So he was an adversary to Israel all the days of Solomon, along with the evil that Hadad did; and he abhorred Israel and reigned over Aram. (vv. 24–25)

Hounds in the Alley

When we seek to elude God by walking down the dark streets of defiance, He has ways of calling dogs from all sorts of alleys. Often we don't even know they're there. They just sort of skulk in the shadows, gnawing on some garbaged bone—until God whistles. Then, like bloodhounds, they're off and running, hot on the scent. Baying and barking, they sniff us out wherever we may be hiding. Tenacious. Tireless. At times, terrifying. These wild dogs may take the form of a memory . . . a face from the past . . . a bankruptcy . . . an illness. When David kept silent about his sin with Bathsheba and the murder of Uriah, God loosed His hounds:

> For day and night Thy hand was heavy upon me;
> My vitality was drained away as with the fever
> heat of summer. (Ps. 32:4)

If you're one of His children skipping footloose and defiant through life, why not give up—before God lets out another hound? Why not do what David did?

> I acknowledged my sin to Thee,
> And my iniquity I did not hide;

> I said, "I will confess my transgressions to the
>   Lord";
> And Thou didst forgive the guilt of my sin.
> (v. 5)
> Then, instead of hiding from the snarling, barking hounds,
> you can say with David:
> Thou art my hiding place; Thou dost preserve
> me from trouble; Thou dost surround me with
> songs of deliverance. (v. 7)

C. Internal rebellion (1 Kings 11:26–39). Hadad and Rezon, from Egypt and Damascus, were external threats to the kingdom. However, internal unrest also began to unravel Solomon's reign, as one of Solomon's most trusted men—Jeroboam—rebelled against his king.

> Then Jeroboam the son of Nebat, an Ephraimite of
> Zeredah, Solomon's servant, whose mother's name
> was Zeruah, a widow, also rebelled against the king.
> (v. 26)

Jeroboam was a "valiant warrior" and "industrious," appointed by Solomon to oversee the forced labor for the house of Joseph (v. 28). He was so trusted by Solomon that only the intervention of God could drive a wedge between them—which is exactly what happened. In verses 29–39, God speaks to Jeroboam through His prophet Ahijah, informing him of Solomon's idolatry and defiance and of His plan to divide the kingdom.

> "'But I will take the kingdom from his son's hand and
> give it to you, even ten tribes.... And I will take you,
> and you shall reign over whatever you desire, and
> you shall be king over Israel.'" (vv. 35, 37)

D. Personal frustration (1 Kings 11:40). As if the presence of his adversaries wasn't enough, Solomon encounters immense personal frustration as well.

> Solomon sought therefore to put Jeroboam to death;
> but Jeroboam arose and fled to Egypt to Shishak king
> of Egypt, and he was in Egypt until the death of
> Solomon. (v. 40)

Solomon was one of the richest, most powerful men in history. He was king, yet he felt as helpless as a pawn with regard to Jeroboam. Like a chess piece craftily eluding capture, Jeroboam slipped between Solomon's fingers—to wait in the protected square of Egypt until the time was ripe to move in and checkmate the king.

The Downward Spiral of Defiance

Defiance is a staircase leading to the very basement of spiritual experience. Each spiraling step leads dizzily downward—twisting itself around a tall, vertical "I." The first step is *selfishness:* "I want my own way." The second is *stubbornness:* "I won't quit until I get it." The third, *indifference:* "I don't care who it hurts." The fourth, *resistance:* "I refuse to listen to advice." The final step before the fall is *contempt:* "I don't care about the consequences." You can almost hear the crash in the dark at the bottom of the stairs, can't you? Defiance leads to personal misery (Prov. 13:15) and results in inescapable bondage (5:21–23). The best way to escape the crash is to avoid the basement stairs altogether . . . and wind your life in an upward spiral around Jesus.

 Living Insights

Study One

Defiance—it has been incarnated in Solomon and his refusal to obey. Scripture is full of other accounts where God's men and women have chosen their own way. Can you think of some?

- First, see how many examples you can recall from memory. Second, consult a concordance, study Bible, Bible handbook, and so forth, to expand your list. Look under "sin," "disobedience," "rebellion."
- Then, using the list you've just compiled, write a lesson you've learned next to each entry. Try to put it in a sentence or two. Conclude by praying thoughtfully over this.

 Living Insights

Study Two

Use the following questions to stimulate your thinking. Or, better yet, gather close friends or family together and discuss these as a group.

- Take time to explore each question deeply.
    - How has our culture influenced the "I want my own way" syndrome?
    - What are some subtle ways we manifest the stubborn "I won't quit until I get it" attitude?

Continued on next page

—Why should we care who gets hurt? Why not just look out for our own interests?

—How do we quietly get around listening to the counsel of others?

—What Scriptures come to mind as a result of these questions?

—Can you think of occasions when defiance hasn't led to personal misery? Expand on that.

—How can we become the victims of the very things we pursue?

• Trace back over the recent past. Are there signs of defiance? Are you ready to deal with it? Are you willing to turn over all the turmoil to Christ? Will you accept His forgiveness? If you've never met Christ, talk with God and receive Him now.

Sound Advice from an Old Rebel
Ecclesiastes 11:9–12:7

Osteoporosis...arthritis...arteriosclerosis...angina. Cold, sterile medical terms with Latin roots and antiseptic sounds...diseases of the elderly. Sadly, the autumn years of most lives are not a treeful of fall's flaming colors. Rather, they are scattered shreds of brittleness that crunch dryly under Life's heavy footsteps. Memories, often muted with regret, cluster in little wind-blown piles—"If only time could be turned back...if only I had it to do all over again...if only..." Perhaps the hardest thing to face about old age is not the physical pain, but the guilt connected with feelings of wasted days spent in waywardness and rebellion. Such is the case of Solomon in his old age. Like arthritis rusting away his joints, remorse for his former life creaked from deep inside and ached his every bone. Painfully stiff and inflamed, his autumn days were anything but golden.

I. Solomon's Closing Years (1 Kings 11:40–43)
As the sun westered away on Solomon's life, the self-indulgent pleasures of his earlier years thinned on the horizon. All that remained was the burning memory of his infidelity to God. As brutal reminders of his defiant days, three God-positioned men and their armies cast long shadows across Solomon's deathbed—Hadad from Edom, Rezon from Damascus, and Jeroboam from Israel. Although his forty-year reign was a golden age of peace for Israel, as the sun set on his life, the foreboding clouds of judgment were gathering in turbulent clusters and closing in on him.

II. Solomon's Advice to the Young (Ecclesiastes 11:9–12:7)
In Ecclesiastes, the diary of his latter years, Solomon records his regrets and advises his younger readers.

A. Remember—you are accountable to God (11:9–10).
Characteristically, many lose their sense of physical balance as they grow older. Oftentimes, however, as in the case of Solomon, *spiritual* balance becomes keener.

> Rejoice, young man, during your childhood, and let your heart be pleasant during the days of young manhood. And follow the impulses of your heart and the desires of your eyes. Yet know that God will bring you to judgment for all these things. (v. 9)

The heat of youth's passion is to be tempered with the quenching reality that all of our actions will one day be placed on the unyielding anvil of God's judgment. Consequently, the fleeting prime of our life should be weighed against the permanence of eternity.

37

So, remove vexation from your heart and put away
pain from your body, because childhood and the
prime of life are fleeting. (11:10)
B. Get your priorities on target early (12:1). Most people
tend to put off any kind of commitment until later in life—"I'll
wait till I've had my fling with life, wait till I get older and settle
down, then I'll look into spiritual things a little more." Solomon
advises just the opposite.

Remember also your Creator in the days of your
youth, before the evil days come and the years draw
near when you will say, "I have no delight in them."

Remembering Your Creator

Remembering God was the stern warning to Israel as they
stood on the borders of the Promised Land (Deut. 8:11, 18).
Forgetting Him landed them in the wilderness (Heb. 3:12–19,
1 Cor. 10:1–11). To forget God is to inadvertently leave Him
out of your day-to-day life. It is to work, but to do so without acknowledging Him as both partner and patron of your
business (Col. 3:23). It is to make decisions, but without
consulting Him for direction and approval. James gives
some practical advice on how you can remember God in
your day-to-day plans.

Come now, you who say, "Today or tomorrow,
we shall go to such and such a city, and spend
a year there and engage in business and make
a profit." Yet you do not know what your life
will be like tomorrow. You are just a vapor that
appears for a little while and then vanishes
away. Instead, you ought to say, "If the Lord
wills, we shall live and also do this or that."
(4:13–15)

To remember your Creator is to realize that all good things
in life are handcrafted gifts from God (James 1:17) . . . every
physical blessing, every spiritual blessing, every step, every
breath (Acts 17:28). To forget God is like forgetting the keys
to your car. The tank may be full of gas, the radiator full
of water, the tires full of air, but without the keys, none of
those things will get you anywhere. God is the *key* to everything in life that really matters: every relationship, every
struggle, every decision. The Creator—don't leave home
without Him!

C. Age works against you, not for you (12:2–5). In a vividly poetic way, Solomon describes the stark realities of aging. They are days of darkness and clouds, of weakness and idleness, of poor hearing and light sleeping.

> Before the sun, the light, the moon, and the stars are darkened, and clouds return after the rain; in the day that the watchmen of the house tremble, and mighty men stoop, the grinding ones stand idle because they are few, and those who look through windows grow dim; and the doors on the street are shut as the sound of the grinding mill is low, and one will arise at the sound of the bird, and all the daughters of song will sing softly. (vv. 2–4)

Solomon's tone becomes more sober as he continues his dirge on the plight of the elderly. Fear, impotence, and separation from loved ones are the low notes of old age.

> Furthermore, men are afraid of a high place and of terrors on the road; the almond tree blossoms, the grasshopper drags himself along, and the caperberry is ineffective. For man goes to his eternal home while mourners go about in the street. (v. 5)

D. Death is inevitable—sooner than many think (vv. 6–7). As if from his deathbed, pulling himself up to utter his last words, Solomon looks us straight in the eye and pleads:

> Remember Him before the silver cord is broken and the golden bowl is crushed, the pitcher by the well is shattered and the wheel at the cistern is crushed; then the dust will return to the earth as it was, and the spirit will return to God who gave it. (vv. 6–7)

Like an earthenware pitcher that falls to the ground and is shattered, spilling its water to evaporate into the air, so when we die, our broken bodies will return to the earth and our spirits will return to heaven.

III. Death: No Respecter of Persons

Death—that Grim Reaper—is no respecter of persons. Rich. Poor. Black. White. Male. Female. Old. Young. Flower or weed, stalk or seed, nothing alive is out of the long reach of Death's scythe. None knew that better than H. G. Spafford.

A. An illustration. Spafford was a Christian businessman who lived in Chicago in the 1800s. He had invested heavily in real estate on the shores of Lake Michigan, only to have it destroyed months later in the Chicago Fire of 1871. For weeks, Spafford and his wife helped feed, clothe, comfort, and give shelter to the homeless victims of the fire. Exhausted from the ordeal, they were counseled by a physician to take a long, relaxing trip. Needing to stay on in Chicago, Spafford sent his wife and four daughters ahead of him to Europe. On November 22, however, during the passage over, their ship, the S.S. *Ville du Havre,* was struck by an English vessel and sank in twelve minutes. His wife and young daughters held on desperately to some floating pieces of wreckage, but one by one the weary daughters slipped out of their mother's grasp and into a watery grave. Several days later, the survivors finally landed in Wales, where Mrs. Spafford cabled her husband with the bittersweet news: "Saved alone." Spafford then left by ship to join his bereaved wife. At sea, he penned the words to the now popular hymn:

> When peace, like a river, attendeth my way,
> When sorrows like sea billows roll—
> Whatever my lot, Thou hast taught me to say,
> It is well, it is well with my soul.[1]

B. An application. The hymn, "It Is Well with My Soul," reveals a peace that surpasses all understanding (Phil. 4:7)—a peace that only Jesus can give (John 14:27). Can you face death with that type of peace? Is it well with your soul? Or is your soul troubled at the thought of death, either yours or that of a loved one? If so, Jesus has some comforting words for you.

> "Let not your heart be troubled; believe in God, believe also in Me. In My Father's house are many dwelling places; if it were not so, I would have told you; for I go to prepare a place for you. And if I go and prepare a place for you, I will come again, and receive you to Myself; that where I am, there you may be also." (John 14:1–3)

---

1. Horatio G. Spafford, "It Is Well with My Soul," in *101 Hymn Stories,* by Kenneth W. Osbeck, foreword by J. Stratton Shufelt (Grand Rapids, Mich.: Kregel Publications, 1982), p. 126.

Living Insights

Study One ━━━━━━━━━━━━━━━━━━━━━━━━━━━━━━━━━━━━━━━

Rehoboam was Solomon's carbon copy; for an undisciplined dad cannot raise a disciplined son. Rehoboam is described in 2 Chronicles 10:1–12:16. As you read this passage, jot down traits of Rehoboam that were similar to his dad's. Then go back over Solomon's life and write down each corresponding characteristic with its Scripture reference. Use the following example as a pattern for your study.

Traits of Rehoboam	Verses	Traits of Solomon	Verses
He forsook the law of the Lord.	2 Chron. 12:1	He loved God, except he sacrificed and burned incense on the high places.	1 Kings 3:3

 Living Insights

Study Two ━━━━━━━━━━━━━━━━━━━━━━━━━━━━━━━━━━━━━━━

This lesson was certainly sobering. We were able to glance over Solomon's shoulder as he made some final entries into his diary. Put yourself in his place right now. Enter your thoughts in your diary under the following heading: "If I Had It to Do All Over Again, This Is the Way It Would Be."

- The point of this lesson was clear—the time to walk with God is now, not later. Read the statements below and circle the responses that are true for your life.

  1. Are you walking with God now?

     Yes   No

  2. Are you consciously aware of your accountability to God?

     Yes   No

  3. Would you consider your priorities to be "on target"?

     Yes   No

  4. Are you seeking a godly lifestyle and right thinking *now?*

     Yes   No

Continued on next page

5. How is your walk with God affecting your spouse?

     Positively   Negatively   Unsure

6. How is your walk with God affecting your children?

     Positively   Negatively   Unsure

7. How is your walk with God affecting your close friends?

     Positively   Negatively   Unsure

8. How is your walk with God affecting your roommates?

     Positively   Negatively   Unsure

9. How is your walk with God affecting your fellow workers?

     Positively   Negatively   Unsure

- Jot down some specific areas in your life that you'd like to begin working on. Include some positive ways to implement change. Ask God for strength, patience, and perseverance.

A Plea for Godliness

1 Peter 1:13–16

The Scriptures refer to sheep, lambs, ewes, sheepfolds, and shepherds about six hundred times. With these metaphors the Holy Spirit communicates to us a wealth of images about our relationship with the Lord. One insightful example is found in Isaiah 53:6: "All of us like sheep have gone astray, / Each of us has turned to his own way." Sheep have a habit of wandering from the flock. Often a sheep moves from one clump of grass to another, so enmeshed in each green island of vegetation that no thought is given as to how far it has ventured from the fold. We are all, as the hymnist says, "prone to wander." We have seen it in Solomon; we see it in ourselves. In selfish pursuit of our own desires, we have chosen a way that is far from the Shepherd. And so we wander through life solitary, separated from God. This predisposition to waywardness is a universal tendency. It is our nature—a nature that is fallen, wayward, depraved. Left to itself, this depraved nature strays from everything godly. Just like sheep, the farther we wander, the greater the dangers. In our insatiable search for greener grass, we slip away to permissive pastures. These lead to winding trails of rationalization, which, in turn, lead to the sheer cliffs of rebellion. That's the path Solomon took when he strayed from God. But like a shepherd calling in the darkness for a lost sheep, God called to him twice, but Solomon, standing on the precipice, ignored the plea (1 Kings 11:9–10). You may be on the precipice yourself this very moment. Or on the winding trail leading to it. Or grazing contentedly amid the seductive lushness of the pasture. Wherever, God is cupping His hands and calling you, in a plea for godliness, to come home.

I. The Root of Depravity (Isaiah 64:6)

At the root of depravity is a nature totally alienated from God. As a bad tree cannot produce good fruit (Matt. 7:18), so the depraved roots of our nature can produce nothing that will gain God's approval.

> For all of us have become like one who is unclean,
> And all our righteous deeds are like a filthy garment.
> (Isa. 64:6a)

Regardless of how moral and upstanding we view ourselves, we are all like the leper who has to cry out in the street "Unclean! Unclean!" so that people may get out of the way (Lev. 13:45). Like Cain, we may proudly bring our fruit baskets of good works before the throne of God (compare Gen. 4:2–5 with Heb. 11:4). But they will lay before God in a limp, disgusting pile, like the bandages from putrifying sores.

II. The Fruit of Depravity (Romans 3:10–18, Galatians 2:16–23)

As the love of money is the root of all sorts of evil (1 Tim. 6:10), so depravity gives branch to a variety of ill fruit: immorality, gossip, lying, impure thoughts, violence, thefts, and so forth. Romans 3 is a tesselation of Old Testament passages inlaid to produce a mosaic of our depraved nature. Paul starts with the universal root in verses 10–12: " 'There is none righteous, not even one' " (v. 10), and then points out the specific fruit in verses 13–18: deceit, cursing, bitterness, destruction, misery, no fear of God. In similar fashion, he enumerates the deeds of the flesh in Galatians 5.

> Now the deeds of the flesh are evident, which are: immorality, impurity, sensuality, idolatry, sorcery, enmities, strife, jealousy, outbursts of anger, disputes, dissensions, factions, envying, drunkenness, carousing, and things like these, of which I forewarn you just as I have forewarned you that those who practice such things shall not inherit the kingdom of God. (vv. 19–21)

If the nature we are born with is depraved, then the only way to produce fruit that is good in God's eyes is to receive a new nature (Eph. 4:22–24, 5:8–9).

The Fruit of the Spirit

In Galatians 5:22–23a, Paul gives us a taste of the new nature's fruit: "love, joy, peace, patience, kindness, goodness, faithfulness, gentleness, self-control." Do you wish people could be feeding from the Spirit's sweet, refreshing fruit in your life instead of getting cut from the thorns and thistles that may be growing there? Remember the words of Christ: "Grapes are not gathered from thorn bushes, nor figs from thistles" (Matt. 7:16b). If you will ever produce fruit pleasing to Him and nourishing to others, *He* must plant a new nature in your heart (Eph. 2:3, 2 Pet. 1:4). Fruit by any other method is only a wax imitation. And in a world hungering for spiritual reality, who needs more artificial fruit?

III. The Rationalization of Depravity (1 Samuel 15)

There is nothing pretty about our old nature. Sometimes—like with the photo on our driver's license—we deny the resemblance. Other times we rationalize. The mirror of Romans 3:10–18 reflects a nature that is ugly and depraved. When looking into this passage, our natural tendency is to rationalize what we see—"the lighting's too bright" or "everybody looks bad in the morning." A classic example of rationalization is shelved away in 1 Samuel 15. In this chapter, we find a soiled page in Saul's reign over Israel. The Lord had commanded Saul to utterly destroy the Amalekites and all of their possessions because of the way their ancestor Amalek had treated Israel upon their exodus from Egypt (vv. 1–3). Saul's follow-through on this command, however, was less than complete, as he not only spared their king but also kept their choicest goods, being unwilling "to destroy them utterly" (v. 9). When Samuel, God's prophet, came to confront Saul with his failure to obey, Saul squirmed in his sandals and hastily created a flimsy rationalization.

And Saul said, "They have brought them from the Amalekites, for the people spared the best of the sheep and oxen, to sacrifice to the Lord your God; but the rest we have utterly destroyed." (v. 15)

Samuel's response is like a sharp scalpel driven to the root of Saul's rebellious nature.

"Why then did you not obey the voice of the Lord, but rushed upon the spoil and did what was evil in the sight of the Lord? . . .

Has the Lord as much delight in burnt offer-
  ings and sacrifices
As in obeying the voice of the Lord?
Behold, to obey is better than sacrifice,
And to heed than the fat of rams.
For rebellion is as the sin of divination,
And insubordination is as iniquity and idolatry.
Because you have rejected the word of the
  Lord,
He has also rejected you from being king."
(vv. 19, 22–23)

IV. Redemption from Depravity (1 Peter 1:13–16)

Depravity has a gravitational pull that leads downward to rebellion. We have seen it in the lives of Solomon and Saul, as well as in our own. If the righteous nature is ignored, permissiveness results. Permissiveness then leads to rationalization when holiness is ignored. And rationalization leads to rebellion when repentance is ignored. Just as our physical bodies soften and sag when we lapse into inactivity, so our spiritual lives need aerobics of the soul if we are ever to overcome the gravity of our depraved nature. Notice how active the verbs are in the advice Peter gives us regarding godliness.

Therefore, gird your minds for action, keep sober in spirit, fix your hope completely on the grace to be brought to you at the revelation of Jesus Christ. As obedient children, do not be conformed to the former lusts which were yours in your ignorance, but like the Holy One who called you, be holy yourselves also in all your behavior; because it is written, "You shall be holy, for I am holy." (1 Pet. 1:13–16)

The "former lusts" in verse 14 are the fruit of our old nature. And the gravity of that nature continually draws us back there to feed. This

45

tug-of-war between the flesh and the Spirit is hostile and constant (Gal. 5:17). The rope is always taut. Simply becoming a Christian and receiving a new nature does not guarantee victory—at least, not without a struggle. Notice the sweat pour out of verse 13 in the phrases: *"gird* your minds . . . *keep* sober in spirit . . . *fix* your hope" (emphasis added). First Peter 1:13–16 is a call to arms and a plea for godliness—a plea to be like the Holy One who called us.

The Good Shepherd

The One who calls you is the Good Shepherd (see John 10:14–16). He calls in the dark . . . in the fog . . . in the rain. He will scale any mountain and descend into any valley to find you—to bring you back into His arms.

> For thus says the Lord God, "Behold, I Myself will search for My sheep and seek them out. As a shepherd cares for his herd in the day when he is among his scattered sheep, so I will care for My sheep and will deliver them from all the places to which they were scattered on a cloudy and gloomy day. . . . I will feed My flock and I will lead them to rest," declares the Lord God. "I will seek the lost, bring back the scattered, bind up the broken, and strengthen the sick." (Ezek. 34:11–12, 15–16a)

Like sheep, all of us have gone astray. That's our nature—to wander. But it's His nature to seek and save those who are lost . . . to comfort . . . to heal . . . to nourish . . . to hold.

Living Insights

Study One ▬▬▬▬▬▬▬▬▬▬▬▬▬▬▬▬▬▬▬▬▬▬▬▬▬▬▬▬

The central passage in this lesson is 1 Peter 1:13–16. It tells us much about taking the initiative to be holy. On a sheet of paper, copy the following chart. The left column contains key words and phrases from this passage. The center column is for you to define each. Use a dictionary if you must. But better yet, seek to clarify the words and phrases in your own words. Finally, in the right column jot down another portion of Scripture that sheds additional light on that subject. If you get stuck at this point, use your concordance, looking up entries beginning with the key word of the phrase.

Key Words or Phrases	Definitions	Other References
Gird your minds for action		
Keep sober in spirit		
Fix your hope completely		
Grace		
Revelation of Jesus Christ		
As obedient children		
Do not be conformed		
Former lusts		
Ignorance		
Holy One		
Called you		
Behavior		
You shall be holy, for I am holy		

 Living Insights

Study Two ▬▬▬▬▬▬▬▬▬▬▬▬▬▬▬▬▬▬▬▬▬▬▬▬▬▬▬▬

Depravity—willfully choosing to rebel against God. Let's take time to personalize this material. Use the following questions to prompt you to evaluate your life. Look through the entire list and select the thoughts that are most meaningful to you.

● Has permissiveness entered your life? If so, trace back to its beginning. How did it start?

Continued on next page

47

- Did it then lead to rationalization? Are you good at rationalizing? Think of some ways it could have crept into your life.
- Has rationalization reached the point of rebellion? What can you do to keep this from occurring?
- Do you believe your depraved nature is still with you? How does it show itself in your life?
- Does your private life differ from your public life? If so, how? Are the differences good?
- List some ways you can take the initiative to be holy. List practical things that can be implemented right away.
- In your case, does depravity begin in the mind? Are there certain settings that cause your mind greater temptation than others? What are they? What's your battle plan for victory?
- In order to counteract permissiveness, list a few practical ways you will take God seriously this week.
- Counteracting rationalization involves pursuing God vigorously. How will you make this part of your lifestyle?
- Submitting to God willingly counteracts rebellion. Are there areas of your life still not under the Lord's authority? Name them. Will you give them to God? If not, what will it take for you to give them to Him?

Needed: A Godly Mind
Ephesians 6:10–17, 2 Corinthians 10:1–5

The mind is the Gettysburg of a very uncivil war between God and Satan. It is the war-torn battlefield of choice where good and evil square off. It is here that conscience unsheathes its sword to clash against expedience, that conviction bares its arm against temptation, that character raises its flag against corruption. The mind is where every important battle is first fought. Theft occurs in thought before it ever lays hands on its coveted object. Adultery wins in the brain before it ever enters the bedroom. Murder lurks in the dark alleys of the mind before it ever comes out of hiding to actually kill its victim. Ultimately, all of life's battles are either won or lost in the mind. Because the stakes are so high, the strategy to gain control of this territory is keen; the competition on both sides, fierce. Describing the battle of his conversion from atheism to Christianity, C. S. Lewis recollects:

> A young man who wishes to remain a sound Atheist cannot be too careful of his reading. There are traps everywhere—"Bibles laid open, millions of surprises," as Herbert says, "fine nets and strategems." God is, if I may say it, very unscrupulous.[1]

But Satan, too, is cunning in his methods, as Paul says in 2 Corinthians 2:11, "in order that no advantage be taken of us by Satan; for we are not ignorant of his schemes." Nets . . . strategems . . . schemes. The battle is real. God and Satan are vying for the most valuable territory in all the world—your mind.

I. Elements of the Battle (Ephesians 6:10–14)

In Ephesians 6, Paul takes us into the council chamber of heaven, where the war is mapped, enemy movements are charted, and strategies discussed.

A. The battle cry (v. 10). Paul rallies the warriors with these stirring words:

> Finally, be strong in the Lord, and in the strength of His might.

Notice where the strength lies—not in ourselves but "in the Lord . . . [in] His might."

B. The battle strategy (v. 11). Continuing, Paul gives instruction on how to be strong.

> Put on the full armor of God, that you may be able to stand firm against the schemes of the devil.

Note again that it is not *our* armor but the armor *of God* we are to put on. The battle is spiritual; therefore, if the weapons are to be effective, they, too, must be spiritual. When the enemy is an invading bacteria, the defense is white blood cells or penicillin. When the enemy is an invading army, the defense is

1. C. S. Lewis, *Surprised by Joy* (New York, N.Y.: Harcourt Brace Jovanovich, 1955), p. 191.

guns, tanks, and planes. But when the enemy is the devil, the only defense is the armor of God. The exhortation to "stand firm" is highlighted in this verse and stressed again in verses 13 and 14.

C. The battleground (v. 12). Paul now begins unrolling the map of spiritual warfare to reveal the enemy's hiding places.

> For our struggle is not against flesh and blood, but against the rulers, against the powers, against the world forces of this darkness, against the spiritual forces of wickedness in the heavenly places.

Our enemy is not the people who oppose us. They are merely victims of the enemy. The enemy is an organized hierarchy of demonic rulers, powers, and forces of darkness and wickedness whose activities originate in the heavenly places and extend to the whole world.

Standing Firm

In Church history, perhaps the best example of a man standing firm is Martin Luther. On April 18, 1521, at the Diet of Worms, Luther was pressured to recant his then controversial views on Scripture and the Church. However, in a courageous speech to his accusers, he refused to compromise his beliefs: "Here I stand, I cannot do otherwise."[2] Standing firm is the only victorious posture the Christian can assume when confronted by Satan and his emissaries. Are you resisting the devil with Luther's resolve, or are you retreating? It is true that our "adversary, the devil, prowls about like a roaring lion, seeking someone to devour" (1 Pet. 5:8). But when we resist him with the armor of God, he reverts to the cowardly lion he is—and flees (James 4:7).

D. The battle armor (vv. 13–16). Again, Paul emphasizes the necessity to fight fire with fire. In the spiritual battle, spiritual defenses are our only protection.

> Therefore, take up the full armor of God, that you may be able to resist in the evil day, and having done everything, to stand firm. Stand firm therefore, having girded your loins with truth, and having put on the breastplate of righteousness, and having shod your feet with the preparation of the gospel of peace; in

---

2. *Bartlett's Familiar Quotations,* 14th ed., Emily Morison Beck, ed. (Boston, Mass.: Little, Brown and Co., 1968), p. 179.

addition to all, taking up the shield of faith with which
you will be able to extinguish all the flaming missiles
of the evil one.

We are the targets of Satan's offensive. Our minds are in the cross
hairs of his scope. His mission: assassination.

II. The Battle

Just as we would need to be sober and alert if a ravenous lion were
roaming around, so we need that same degree of attention to guard
ourselves against our very real spiritual adversary (1 Pet. 5:8).

A. Satan's schemes. In order to repel our adversary, we must
first know which direction he's coming from. We must spot him
before he pounces on us.

But whom you forgive anything, I forgive also; for
indeed what I have forgiven, if I have forgiven anything, I did it for your sakes in the presence of Christ,
in order that no advantage[3] be taken of us by Satan; for
we are not ignorant of his schemes.[4] (2 Cor. 2:10–11)

One dangerous area of vulnerability is failing to forgive one
another. When we do that, we give Satan an advantage . . . an
open door . . . an entrance. We lay out a welcome mat for him
in another area—prolonged anger.

Be angry, and yet do not sin; do not let the sun go
down on your anger, and do not give the devil an
opportunity. (Eph. 4:26–27)

Unresolved personal conflicts are part of Satan's schemes. He
knows that if bitterness fills our minds, there will be little room
for thoughts of God.

> ### The Battle Zone of the Mind
> The mind will be occupied either with the things of God
> or with things that delight the devil. As C. S. Lewis rightly
> observed: "There is no neutral ground in the universe:
> every square inch, every split second, is claimed by God
> and counterclaimed by Satan."[5] Whose flag is planted in
> your mind? If your mind is filled with anger and bitterness,
> the colors flying indicate that the territory is occupied by

---

3. The word *advantage* is from the Greek *pleonekteō*, meaning "to take advantage of, to gain,
to overreach, to outwit." In the New Testament, it is found only in 2 Corinthians 2:11, 7:2,
12:17–18, and 1 Thessalonians 4:6.

4. The word *schemes* is from the Greek *noēma*, meaning "mind" or "thought." Compare
2 Corinthians 2:11 and 11:3 with 10:5.

5. C. S. Lewis, *Christian Reflections* (Grand Rapids, Mich.: William B. Eerdmans Publishing Co.,
1967), p. 33.

the enemy. Burn that flag, won't you? Bury the bitterness. Let love do its spadework to cover the multitude of sins committed against you by that offending person. And raise a new flag over that war-ravaged territory!

B. Satan's target. Like birds picking up seeds, keeping the kernels from taking root along the roadside, Satan snatches the gospel away and prevents it from taking root in our minds (compare Luke 8:5 with Luke 8:11–12).

> And even if our gospel is veiled, it is veiled to those who are perishing, in whose case the god of this world has blinded the minds of the unbelieving, that they might not see the light of the gospel of the glory of Christ, who is the image of God. (2 Cor. 4:3–4)

The natural man has a flock of Satan's messengers surrounding him so that when a seed of God's truth falls anywhere near him, it is pecked to death—before it ever has a chance to take root.

C. Satan besieged. In order for Christ to conquer the territory of a blinded and imprisoned mind, He must penetrate the walls built by Satan. And in doing so, He must use the right weaponry.

> For though we walk in the flesh, we do not war according to the flesh, for the weapons of our warfare are not of the flesh, but divinely powerful for the destruction of fortresses. (2 Cor. 10:3–4)

The battle targets are described, metaphorically, as "fortresses." This word picture is drawn from ancient biblical history, when strategic cities were surrounded by fortified walls of defense. Within these walls were carefully placed towers, built higher than the highest point of the surrounding wall. They served as observation posts for the battle strategists, who were flanked by buglers who sent signals to the soldiers. For a city to be conquered, the walls had to be scaled, the towers seized, and the strategists captured. For a mind to become captive to Christ, the walls and towers erected by Satan must also be penetrated.

Penetrating the Mental Fortress

God destroys Satan's fortress by storming the walls of "speculations" and scaling the towers of "every lofty thing raised up against the knowledge of God" (2 Cor. 10:5). The word *speculations* comes from the Greek word *logismos,* meaning "thought" or "reasonings." We get our word *logic* from the same root. But the logic God uses to penetrate our mental walls is totally opposite from the world's.

For the word of the cross is to those who are perishing foolishness, but to us who are being saved it is the power of God. For it is written,

> "I will destroy the wisdom of the wise,
> And the cleverness of the clever I
> will set aside."

Where is the wise man? Where is the scribe? Where is the debater of this age? Has not God made foolish the wisdom of the world? For since in the wisdom of God the world through its wisdom did not come to know God, God was well-pleased through the foolishness of the message preached to save those who believe. (1 Cor. 1:18–21)

The logic of God is sacrificial love; His battering ram, a bloodstained cross.

III. Wielding Our Weapons

Nearly all the weapons listed in Ephesians 6 are defensive—breastplate, shield, helmet. The only offensive one is found at the tail end of the list in verse 17: "the sword of the Spirit, which is the word of God." Like the sword Excalibur in the Arthurian legends, the Word of God carries with it a certain enchantment. It cuts and penetrates like no earthly weapon.

> For the word of God is living and active and sharper than
> any two-edged sword, and piercing as far as the division
> of soul and spirit, of both joints and marrow, and able to
> judge the thoughts and intentions of the heart. (Heb. 4:12)

With the battering ram of the cross and the sword of the Spirit, Satan's fortresses can be destroyed; the enemy, evicted. Thoughts, once enslaved, can be emancipated to serve the Lord Jesus—"and you shall know the truth, and the truth shall make you free" (John 8:32).

Continued on next page

Living Insights

Study One ▬▬▬▬▬▬▬▬▬▬▬▬▬▬▬▬▬▬▬▬▬▬▬▬▬▬▬▬▬▬▬

One need only casually glance through the Bible to see the vital importance of a godly mind. It is threaded through the entire fabric of Scripture. Let's use the New Testament as an example. Take one minute for each book, and write down a thought on godliness or the mind from each reference given.

References	Observations	References	Observations
Matt. 22:37		1 Tim. 6:11	
Mark 8:33		2 Tim. 3:12	
Luke 8:15		Titus 2:11–14	
John 14:21		Philem. 6	
Acts 17:11		Heb. 8:10	
Rom. 12:2		James 3:13	
1 Cor. 2:16		1 Pet. 1:14–15	
2 Cor. 4:3–4		2 Pet. 1:2–3	
Gal. 6:9		1 John 2:29	
Eph. 4:23		2 John 4	
Phil. 2:3		3 John 11	
Col. 3:2		Jude 20–21	
1 Thess. 2:10–12		Rev. 22:11	
2 Thess. 1:11–12			

 Living Insights

Study Two ▬▬▬▬▬▬▬▬▬▬▬▬▬▬▬▬▬▬▬▬▬▬▬▬▬▬▬▬▬▬▬

Write a candid letter to God. Write first about your depravity, and confess to Him your areas of shortcoming. Perhaps they are dishonesty, deception, anger, your tongue, selfishness, lust, greed, impatience, sensuality, pride, or jealousy. Next, write about rationalization. What is it? It might be blame, justification, lies, comparisons, compromises, habits, reputation, fear, insecurity, bitterness, revenge, or defensiveness.

Books for Probing Further

For Solomon, life was an all-you-can-eat buffet at the finest of restaurants. Daily, he dined on a smorgasbord of culinary and sexual delights, power and politics, wisdom and wealth, art and architecture. From appetizers to desserts, there was no tantalizing experience out of his reach—nothing on life's menu too pricy for his tastes. In his own words: "All that my eyes desired I did not refuse them. I did not withhold my heart from any pleasure" (Eccles. 2:10a). Ironically, his heart was the one that was handed the tab. It picked up the bill for a lifetime of overindulgent pleasure. The tab was a scathing sum total of his life by God: "His heart was not wholly devoted to the Lord his God, as the heart of David his father had been" (1 Kings 11:4). His was a heart with something missing—something essential, something eternal.

In his book *The Problem of Pain,* C. S. Lewis noted that the "soul has a curious shape because it is a hollow made to fit a particular swelling in the infinite contours of the divine substance."[1] It is a hollow made to be filled by God, like glove and hand, shoe and foot, lock and key. Yet Solomon sought to fill that hollow with everything earthly, nothing divine. It is no wonder nothing fit . . . nothing lasted . . . nothing satisfied. It is no wonder his later years were years of misery. He was a restless man, going from woman to woman, project to project, pleasure to pleasure.

Is your heart, like Solomon's, *restless?* In his *Confessions,* Augustine bares his heart before God: "You have made us for yourself, and our hearts are restless till they find their rest in you."[2] Maybe you're seeking rest in the wrong pastures. Maybe you're spending too much time looking for greener grass and not enough time looking for your Shepherd. Is your heart, like Solomon's, *unfulfilled?* Maybe you're filling it with the wrong things—experiences that titillate the tastebuds but don't stick to your spiritual ribs. Essentially, Solomon's problem wasn't wine, women, and song. Or wealth. Or power. It was a problem of the heart.

I hope our studies on Solomon have convinced you of the importance of maintaining a close relationship with God. Nothing else can take His place in your heart. Nothing. And I hope you have the opportunity to read the books listed on the following pages. I think they will go a long way in helping you develop a heart that beats for God.

1. C. S. Lewis, *The Problem of Pain* (New York, N.Y.: Macmillan Co., 1970), p. 147.

2. *The Confessions of Augustine in Modern English,* ed. Sherwood E. Wirt (Grand Rapids, Mich.: Zondervan Publishing House, 1986), p. 1.

Briscoe, Stuart D. *Playing by the Rules.* Old Tappan, N. J.: Fleming H. Revell Co., 1986. Briscoe answers the question: What do the Ten Commandments mean for us today? He examines each commandment, applying it to today's issues of life and faith. From placing God first and foremost in our lives to preventing present-day idolatry, the author's advice is precisely what Solomon needed to get back on track with God, and precisely what we need to hear today.

Lewis, C. S. *The Screwtape Letters.* New York, N.Y.: Macmillan Co., 1960. Our last lesson dealt with schemes of Satan in the battle for our minds and hearts. Few books have dealt with this subject as creatively and profoundly as *The Screwtape Letters.* A milestone in the history of popular theology, this book is widely recognized as Lewis's greatest work. Cast in the form of letters from young apprentice devil Wormwood to elderly Uncle Screwtape, the book is unparalleled in its wit and wisdom.

MacDonald, Gordon. *Ordering Your Private World.* Nashville, Tenn.: Thomas Nelson Publishers, 1984. Solomon's public life was filled with order and opulence. His private life, however, was crammed with chaos and decadence. For him, *Ordering Your Private World* was just what the doctor would have ordered. In this book, MacDonald writes with the clear-headed simplicity and idealism of a prophet, with the straight-shooting realism of a businessman, and yet with the tender compassion of a shepherd.

————. *Restoring Your Spiritual Passion.* Nashville, Tenn.: Thomas Nelson Publishers, 1986. Like Solomon, we are working harder, playing longer, buying more, and yet we are enjoying life less and less. Why there is so much dissatisfaction in our lives is the topic of MacDonald's excellent book. *Restoring Your Spiritual Passion* will give you practical steps to escape the pervasive sense of spiritual and psychic tiredness that may have settled into your life. It will reopen the "rivers of living water" and help quench your inner thirst.

Swindoll, Charles R. *Living on the Ragged Edge.* Waco, Tex.: Word Books, 1985. Exploring Solomon's ancient journal, Ecclesiastes, the author offers new insights into the young king's quest to find pleasure in life. In a world where success is measured by fame, fortune, and the number of executive ulcers we accumulate, this book offers hope to all of us caught in the rat race along life's ragged edge.

White, John. *The Golden Cow.* Downers Grove, Ill.: InterVarsity Press, 1979. Materialism and its hungry sister hedonism ate Solomon's spiritual lunch, one bite at a time. By the end of his life he was left with an empty lunch pail and a lot of crumpled wax paper—spiritually starved. In this convicting book, White seeks to bring material things into proper perspective. He asks the penetrating question: Is it possible that the church today has begun worshiping the golden cow of materialism and success?

Acknowledgments

Insight for Living is grateful for permission to quote from the following sources:

Schaeffer, Franky. *Addicted to Mediocrity: 20th Century Christians and the Arts.* Westchester, Ill.: Good News Publishers/Crossway Books, 1981.

Spafford, Horatio G. "It Is Well with My Soul." In *101 Hymn Stories,* by Kenneth W. Osbeck. Foreword by J. Stratton Shufelt. Grand Rapids, Mich.: Kregel Publications, 1982.

Stevenson, Burton E., ed. *The Home Book of Quotations; Classical and Modern.* 10th ed. 1967. Reprint. New York, N.Y.: Dodd, Mead and Co., 1984.

Insight for Living
Cassette Tapes
SOLOMON

The Bible's wisest fool, Solomon stands as a mute reminder that a great beginning is no guarantee of a great ending. No man began with more promise than Solomon. But, as these studies reveal, the man drifted and finally defected ... as do many today. The first six studies take us on a biographical field trip to observe this erosion in action. The last two studies are soul conservation projects from the New Testament to prevent this erosion from taking place in your own life. You'll find straight talk about temptation, sensuality, defiance, and cynicism in these messages. Hopefully you'll also find sufficient warnings to help you stay true. Let him who thinks he stands take heed!

			U.S.	Canadian
SOL	CS	Cassette series—includes album cover	$23.75	$30.00
		Individual cassettes—include messages		
		A and B	5.00	6.35

These prices are effective as of December 1986 and are subject to change without notice.

SOL 1-A: ***Stepping into Big Sandals***
1 Kings 1, 2 Chronicles 1–9
B: ***Solomon in Living Color***
Selected Scripture

SOL 2-A: ***Signs of Erosion***
Selected Scripture
B: ***When the Heart Is Turned Away***
1 Kings 11:1–13

SOL 3-A: ***How God Deals with Defiance***
1 Kings 11:9–40
B: ***Sound Advice from an Old Rebel***
Ecclesiastes 11:9–12:7

SOL 4-A: ***A Plea for Godliness****
1 Peter 1:13–16
B: ***Needed: A Godly Mind****
Ephesians 6:10–17, 2 Corinthians 10:1–5

*These messages were not a part of the original series but are compatible with it.

Ordering Information

U.S. ordering information: You are welcome to use our toll-free number (for Visa and MasterCard orders only) between the hours of 8:30 A.M. and 4:00 P.M., Pacific time, Monday through Friday. The number is **(800) 772-8888.** This number may be used anywhere in the continental United States excluding California, Hawaii, and Alaska. Orders from those areas are handled through our Sales Department at **(714) 870-9161.** We are unable to accept collect calls.

Your order will be processed promptly. We ask that you allow four to six weeks for delivery by fourth-class mail. If you wish your order to be shipped first-class, please add 10 percent of the total order cost (not including California sales tax) for shipping and handling.

Canadian ordering information: Your order will be processed promptly. We ask that you allow approximately four weeks for delivery by first-class mail to the U.S./Canadian border. All orders will be shipped from our office in Fullerton, California. For our listeners in British Columbia, a 7 percent sales tax must be added to the total of all tape orders (not including first-class postage). For further information, please contact our office at **(604) 272-5811.**

Payment options: We accept personal checks, money orders, Visa, and MasterCard in payment for materials ordered. Unfortunately, we are unable to offer invoicing or COD orders. If the amount of your check or money order is less than the amount of your purchase, your check will be returned so that you may place your order again with the correct amount. All orders must be paid in full before shipment can be made.

Returned checks: There is a $10 charge for any returned check (regardless of the amount of your order) to cover processing and invoicing.

Guarantee: Our tapes are guaranteed for ninety days against faulty performance or breakage due to a defect in the tape. For best results, please be sure your tape recorder is in good operating condition and is cleaned regularly.

Mail your order to one of the following addresses:

Insight for Living	Insight for Living Ministries
Sales Department	Post Office Box 2510
Post Office Box 4444	Vancouver, BC
Fullerton, CA 92634	Canada V6B 3W7

Quantity discounts and gift certificates are available upon request.

Overseas ordering information is provided on the reverse side of the order form.

Order Form

Please send me the following cassette tapes:

The current series: ☐ SOL CS Solomon

Individual cassettes: ☐ SOL 1 ☐ SOL 2 ☐ SOL 3 ☐ SOL 4

I am enclosing:

$_____   To purchase the cassette series for $23.75 (in Canada $30.00*) which includes the album cover

$_____   To purchase individual tapes at $5.00 each (in Canada $6.35*)

$_____   Total of purchases

$_____   If the order will be delivered in California, please add 6 percent sales tax

$_____   U.S. residents please add 10 percent for first-class shipping and handling if desired

$_____   *British Columbia residents please add 7 percent sales tax

$_____   Canadian residents please add 6 percent for postage

$_____   **Overseas residents please add appropriate postage** (See postage chart under "Overseas Ordering Information.")

$_____   As a gift to the Insight for Living radio ministry for which a tax-deductible receipt will be issued

$_____   **Total amount due (Please do not send cash.)**

Form of payment:

☐ Check or money order made payable to Insight for Living

☐ Credit card (Visa or MasterCard only)

If there is a balance: ☐ apply it as a donation ☐ please refund

---

Credit card purchases:

☐ Visa ☐ MasterCard number _____

Expiration date _____

Signature _____

We cannot process your credit card purchase without your signature.

Name _____

Address _____

_____

City _____

State/Province _____ Zip/Postal code _____

Country _____

Telephone (___) _____ Radio station ___ ___ ___ ___

Should questions arise concerning your order, we may need to contact you.

Overseas Ordering Information

If you do not live in the United States or Canada, please note the following information. This will ensure efficient processing of your request.

Estimated time of delivery: We ask that you allow approximately twelve to sixteen weeks for delivery by surface mail. If you would like your order sent airmail, the length of delivery may be reduced. All orders will be shipped from our office in Fullerton, California.

Payment options: Due to fluctuating currency rates, we can accept only personal checks made payable in U.S. funds, international money orders, Visa, and MasterCard in payment for materials ordered. If the amount of your check or money order is less than the amount of your purchase, your check will be returned so that you may place your order again with the correct amount. All orders must be paid in full before shipment can be made.

Returned checks: There is a $10 charge for any returned check (regardless of the amount of your order) to cover processing and invoicing.

Postage and handling: Please add to the amount of purchase the postage cost for the service you desire. All orders must include postage based on the chart below.

Purchase Amount		Surface Postage	Airmail Postage
From	To	Percentage of Order	Percentage of Order
$ .01	$15.00	40%	75%
15.01	75.00	25%	45%
75.01	or more	15%	40%

Guarantee: Our tapes are guaranteed for ninety days against faulty performance or breakage due to a defect in the tape. For best results, please be sure your tape recorder is in good operating condition and is cleaned regularly.

Mail your order or inquiry to the following address:

Insight for Living
Sales Department
Post Office Box 4444
Fullerton, CA 92634

Quantity discounts and gift certificates are available upon request.